Debrett's

DINNER PARTY
COOKBOOK

ANTOINETTE SAVILL

D1280055

DEBRETT'S PEERAGE LIMITED
LONDON · NEW YORK · SYDNEY · PERTH W.A.

Copyright © Antoinette Savill 1986

ISBN 0 905649 85 0

Published by Debrett's Peerage Limited,
73 – 77 Britannia Road, London SW6 2JR

Represented by:
Michael Joseph Limited
27 Wright's Lane
Kensington
London W8

Distributed by:
TBL Book Distribution Services
17 – 32 Nelson Way
Tuscan Trading Estate
Camberley
Surrey

Typeset by Holywell Press Ltd, Oxford
Printed and bound in Great Britain at the Bath Press

FOREWORD

In the past year I have had a wonderful time cooking in the South of France and London. I became very interested in Nouvelle Cuisine and experimented as much as possible whilst working for the De Rothschild family. Since then I have cooked in Long Island and New York.

I have tried to blend traditional cooking with some of the excitement of Nouvelle Cuisine and to adapt this art form into something much quicker and easier for everybody.

I would like to thank everybody who helped me throughout the book, especially Nicky who has displayed such a wealth of imagination and humour in her superb cartoons. Equally a huge thank you to Graham who is now working for the Curzon Wine Co in London. He has managed to spare a little time from his wine tasting to write five informative and amusing pieces on wines and port.

Also my thanks to Caroline, Lucinda and Joslyn for all their help and last but not least, my mother, without whom I would never have completed this book.

CURZON CHAMPAGNE

The Perfect Start to a Debrett Dinner Party

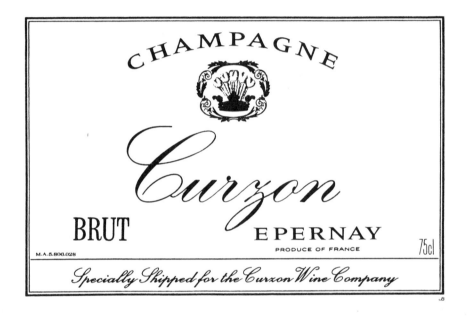

Prepared for us by a small family concern in Epernay,
this light, yet full-flavoured champagne benefits from
a high percentage of Chardonnay grapes.

Available from the Curzon Wine Company,
11 Curzon Street, Mayfair, London W1

Telephone 499 3327 to place your order

Free delivery in Central London

CONTENTS

Lady of the Night

A lot of people have been asking me what they can do for their drinks parties this year. So here are some ideas for delicious cocktails and lots of goodies to give your friends before they rush off to yet another drinks party!

Luscious Lucinda

5 strawberries
Juice of one orange
Juice of half a lemon

1 teaspoon sugar
2 measures white rum

Place the ingredients in a blender with 4 ice cubes and blend until smooth. Pour into a highball glass and decorate with a strawberry on the side of the glass.

Lady of the Night

3 measures apple juice
Juice of half a lemon
1 dash of grenadine

2 measures vodka
Ginger Ale

Mix ingredients with the ice and pour into a tumbler, top it up with ginger ale. Decorate with slices of apple.

The Vicar's Daughter

Half a banana
Juice of one lemon

Juice of one orange
2 measures of rum

Blend ingredients with 4 – 5 ice cubes until smooth.

Cocktails concocted by Charles Savill.

Cocktail Nibbles

Ham and Pâté Rolls

Serves twelve

8 slices of square pre-packed Virginia ham
1 tube (90g) pâté de fois gras
medium sweet sherry
8 slices of fresh brown bread, very thinly cut
butter

Remove the crusts from the bread, roll out firmly with a rolling pin, and lightly butter each slice. Lay a slice of ham on each piece of bread. Mix the sherry with the pâté and spread over the ham and roll up as tightly as possible.

Cut into 3 – 4 mini rolls and keep covered until needed.

Roquefort Cheese Balls

Serves twelve

1 lb (450 g) Roquefort cheese
5 fl oz (150 ml) double cream
black pepper
8 oz (225g) walnuts
cocktail sticks

Remove any rinds from the cheese and crumble into an electric blender, or beat with a wooden spoon in a mixing bowl, with double cream and black pepper.

Roll a teaspoon of the mixture in the palm of your hand and then roll it in a plate of crushed walnuts. Arrange them on a tray with plenty of cocktail sticks.

Mange-Touts Delights

Serves twelve

I was offered a plate of mange-touts with cream cheese at the General Trading Company, at the launching of my first cook book; I thought they were so delicious that I promptly used them at my next cocktail party!

8 oz (225 g) young unblemished mange-touts
8 oz (225 g) cream cheese
¼ pint (150 ml) double cream
few drops of tabasco
salt and pepper
half a red pepper blanched in boiling water

Trim the mange-touts and carefully open them up and remove any tiny peas.

Mix the cheese, tabasco, seasoning and cream together and pipe into each mange-tout. Place a very small strip of red pepper along the cream cheese. Serve in a pinwheel pattern.

Sauté Spiced Nuts

Serves twelve

8 oz (225 g) blanched almonds and whole nuts
2 tablespoons butter
½ teaspoon salt
2 teaspoons ginger and curry powder mixed together

Combine the nuts and sauté them in the butter and spices until golden brown. Drain on absorbent paper and sprinkle with salt. Serve hot or cold.

Prawn Croustades

Serves twelve

These croustades are available in all good delicatessens and keep for ages if unopened.

1 packet of 24 ready-made croustades
8 oz (225 g) shrimps or prawns
1 oz (25 g) butter
1 oz (25 g) flour
black pepper
half a teaspoon each of ginger, curry, coriander and cardamon powders
¼ pint (150 ml) double cream

Melt the butter in a saucepan and beat in the flour and spices. Stir in the prawns for a minute or two and gradually add the cream, beating until you have a smooth sauce. Season according to taste and spoon into the croustades. Heat through and serve immediately before they go soggy.

Cocktail Vol-au-Vents

Each quantity serves twelve

Here we have a pretty combination of colours. I usually arrange them in a chess board pattern for maximum effect.

Recipe 1	Recipe 2
24 cocktail vol-au-vents	24 cocktail vol-au-vents
8 oz (225 g) cream cheese	½ lb (225 g) ready-made
¼ pint (150 ml) double cream,	taramasalata
whipped	¼ pint (150 ml) double cream,
salt and pepper	whipped
3 oz (75 g) red Danish lumpfish	salt and pepper
or caviar	3 oz (75 g) black Danish lumpfish
	or caviar

Bake the vol-au-vents according to the instructions and when they are cold, fill them with the above mixtures and decorate each one with a little lumpfish or caviar.

Recipe 1: Combine cream cheese, salt and pepper with the cream.

Recipe 2: Combine taramasalata with the seasoning and the cream.

Keep both mixtures chilled until needed.

Peanut Butter Sticks

Allow 2 or 3 sticks per person

1 small loaf, thinly sliced brown bread
1 jar crunchy peanut butter
hazelnut oil

Remove the crusts from the bread. Roll out the bread with a rolling pin until very thin. Spread with peanut butter and roll up very tightly. Cut in half.

Heat the oil in a frying pan until boiling and fry the peanut sticks one at a time for about 20 seconds on each side so that they are brown and crispy. Drain on absorbent paper and keep warm until needed.

Soupercook!

Pear Vichyssoise

Serves six

Don't be filled with horror at the thought of a fruity soup! The flavour is so subtle and fine that you will be instantly converted.

3 ripe, juicy pears, peeled and diced into a little lemon juice
half a small onion, finely chopped
2 leeks, cleaned and trimmed, use white part only, finely chopped
1 pint (600 ml) strong chicken stock
1 pint (600 ml) single cream
salt, pepper and nutmeg
2oz (50 g) butter
Chopped chives to decorate

Gently sauté the onion in the butter with the leeks; do not brown them. Pour over the stock and simmer for 20 minutes. Cool the soup and liquidise the stock with the pears and the cream. Season according to taste and chill in the freezer until ready to serve. Decorate with chopped chives.

Mango and Orange Soup

Serves six

The soup needs to be very cold for maximum effect. It is bright and colourful and so is an ideal starter for a summer dinner party.

1 large orange
3 ripe mangoes, peeled and sliced
1 pint (600 ml) fresh or frozen concentrated orange juice diluted as
    instructed
½ pint (300 ml) lukewarm, strong, fresh chicken stock
½ pint (300 ml) Moselle
salt and freshly ground pepper
1 large orange, finely sliced for decoration
freshly chopped chervil to decorate

Finely grate the orange skin and scrape the zest into the stock. Purée the mangoes with the stock, the Moselle and orange juice. Pour the soup into a tureen. Season according to taste, cover and chill for as long as possible. Decorate with slices of orange and sprinkle with chervil.

Leek and Asparagus Soup

Serves ten – twelve. Half the quantity for six

Frozen or tinned asparagus will do perfectly well for this soup, but the flavour of fresh asparagus is so much better.

2lb (900 g) washed, trimmed leeks
4 oz (100 g) butter
1 pint (600 ml) milk
2 pints (1200 ml) chicken stock
½ pint (300 ml) single cream
1lb (450g) asparagus tips, blanched
salt and pepper
chopped parsley and croutons to decorate
freshly grated nutmeg

Chop and sauté the leeks for 10 minutes in the butter. Pour over the stock and simmer for a further 10 minutes. Over low heat, poach the asparagus in the milk and leave to infuse for 10 minutes. Combine the asparagus and milk with the stock and leeks. When the mixture is cold, liquidise the soup, and season according to taste with the nutmeg, salt and pepper.

Chill the soup for as long as possible and decorate with swirls of cream, the parsley and croutons.

Sara's Tuna Fish Soup

Serves eight

When Sara gave me this soup at a dinner party I thought it was a frightfully smart seafood soup. Great was my surprise when I discovered it was merely tuna fish and tomato juice!

1 litre box tomato juice
7 oz (198 g) tin tuna fish in brine
½ onion, very finely chopped
2 oz (50 g) butter
8 oz (225 g) shrimps
salt, pepper and cayenne
¼ pint (300 ml) double cream
chopped parsley

Slowly cook the onion in the butter until soft and transparent. Stir in the tuna fish and break it up as much as possible; stir in the tomato juice and season with a little sprinkling of cayenne, salt and pepper. Cook the soup for 10 minutes and add the shrimps. Simmer for a further 5 minutes and serve decorated with swirls of cream and chopped parsley.

Prosciutto and Cheese Rolls

Serves six

½ lb (225 g) cream cheese
½ lb (225 g) thinly sliced prosciutto (Parma Ham)
halved fresh figs

Divide the cream cheese into 12 sausage shape portions and roll each slice of prosciutto to enclose the cheese. Trim the edges and keep under clingfilm in the refrigerator for at least 1 hour.

Serve the prosciutto rolls on individual plates with as many figs as you like.

Cold Starters

Hazelnut Pâte Croutons Salad

Serves six

Trying my hand at nouvelle cuisine, I came up with this idea. You can make the croutons in advance and keep in an air-tight container. The vinaigrette and pâté can be made well in advance and refrigerated.

Salad

Curly endive
Radicchio
18 fresh asparagus tips
2 raw carrots, cut into very fine
  matchsticks

Croutons

6 slices brown bread
6 oz (175 g) pâté de fois gras
4 dessertspoons roasted, peeled,
  chopped hazelnuts
hazelnut oil

Vinaigrette

4 tablespoons hazelnut or walnut oil
1 teaspoon Dijon mustard
1 tablespoon wine vinegar
salt and pepper

Mix all the ingredients together for the vinaigrette and shake well. Keep chilled.

Make the croutons: Cut 4 heart shapes out of each slice of bread. Heat the hazelnut oil and fry the croutons until golden brown. Drain on absorbent paper. Mix the pâté with the hazelnuts and keep chilled. Before serving, spread the pâté on each crouton.

Wash and dry the salad leaves and arrange them on 6 small plates. Boil the asparagus in salted water for 10 minutes and drain. Arrange the warm asparagus over the salad and pour over the salad dressing. Arrange the croutons on the salad and sprinkle with the raw carrots.

Terrine de Legumes with Tomato Coulis

Serves six

The contrast of the green vegetables in the creamy coloured terrine, against the soft red colour of the sauce makes this a superb dish. The recipe was kindly donated by Renné Carrot, Chef of the restaurant Chez Mireille, Monaco.

4 oz (125 g) baby mange-touts
4 oz (125 g) haricot verts
4 oz (125 g) petit pois
5 eggs
3 oz (75 g) Jockey cream cheese
3 oz (75 g) grated gruyère
1 tablespoon chopped parsley
salt, pepper and nutmeg
butter to grease terrine tin
Bakewell paper to line tin

Tomato Coulis

1 lb (450 g) fresh or tinned
   tomatoes
Chopped herbs, (thyme and
   oregano)
salt and pepper
2 oz (50 g) butter

Set oven at 350°F (180°C, Gas 4). Grease and line a 9 inch (23 cm) terrine tin. Clean and trim the vegetables and blanch them all separately in salted boiling water for a few minutes. Take out the vegetables and drain them on a clean towel.

Beat the eggs with the seasoning and nutmeg, incorporate the cream cheese, gruyère and parsley. Butter the loaf tin and gradually layer the egg mixture with the vegetables until full. Cook in a bain-marie for 40 – 50 minutes and leave to cool. Chill in the refrigerator, turn out the terrine and continue to keep it chilled.

To make the tomato coulis: cook the tomatoes in the butter with the herbs and seasoning until soft, sieve or purée the tomatoes until smooth and then chill until needed.

To assemble: pour the sauce on to each plate. Cut 6 slices of terrine and place them in the centre of the sauce and decorate.

Avocado in Redcurrant Vinaigrette

Serves eight

This is my all-time favourite! I use it at every dinner party because it is so colourful, delicious and unusual, and most of all because it is so quick.

4 ripe avocados, peeled, cut in half and sliced lengthwise
juice of 1 lemon
1 lb (450 g) redcurrants, cooked in a little water until soft
sugar to taste
½ pint (300 ml) vinaigrette, made with white wine vinegar
8 small bunches of redcurrants
8 small sprigs fresh mint for decoration

Make the vinaigrette in a blender so that it is very thick. Purée the redcurrants with the vinaigrette and add the sugar to taste. Chill.

Spoon the sauce on to each plate and arrange the slices of avocado in a fan shape in the centre of each plate. Gently brush a little lemon over the avocado slices to prevent them from colouring.

Decorate with the redcurrants and mint.

Ham and Watercress Mousse

Serves eight

Here is another mousse that looks super as part of a buffet.

¾ lb (350 g) cooked ham
1 tin jellied consommé
½ pint (300 ml) whipped cream
½ oz (11g) gelatine dissolved in water (optional)
1 dessertspoon Cognac
1 teaspoon Dijon mustard
a little Worcestershire sauce
salt and pepper
3 bunches washed watercress
a little oil

Allow 6 hours or more for the mousse to set in a cold refrigerator. If you need the mousse in a shorter time, add the gelatine to the consommé.

Trim 2 bunches of watercress and chop finely. Liquidise the ham with the consommé, add the Cognac, mustard, Worcestershire sauce and season to taste. Stiffly whip the cream and fold into the ham mixture. Fold in the watercress and fill an oiled 9 inch (23 cm) ring mould with the mixture.

Chill for several hours until the mousse has set. Dip the ring in hot water and turn the mousse out on to a plate and decorate with the remaining watercress. Keep refrigerated until needed.

Little Vegetable Tartlets and Mint Hollandaise Sauce

Serves six

This is also a delightful way of presenting vegetables with roast meat at a smart dinner party.

1 packet frozen shortcrust pastry (13.5 oz, 365 g)

Mint Hollandaise Sauce

4 egg yolks
6 oz (175 g) boiling melted butter
1 dessertspoon lemon juice
fresh mint, or fresh tarragon for
   a tarragon hollandaise
salt and pepper

Vegetables

baby carrots, cut into tiny strips
young haricots verts cut into
   similar lengths
little cauliflower florets

Roll out the shortcrust pastry on a floured board. Make 12 tartlets and bake blind until crispy. Cook each of the vegetables separately in salted boiling water. They must be crunchy. Keep them warm and make the hollandaise sauce.

Mix the eggs with the lemon juice, mint leaves, salt and pepper in a magimix and pour in the boiling butter with the machine running until the sauce is thick.

Fill each warm tartlet with warm vegetables and pour over a little sauce. Serve the rest of the sauce around the tartlets. Decorate with some fresh mint.

Hot Starters

Vegetable Timbales in Beurre Blanc

Serves eight

The most important thing here is the decoration around the timbales. I usually use broccoli florets or asparagus tips.

  8 dariol moulds or ramekins, the bottoms lined with a buttered circle
      of greaseproof paper
  cooked vegetables for decoration, kept warm
  3 eggs
  8 fl oz (225 ml) single cream
  2 cups cooked, purée vegetables, eg: broccoli, asparagus or spinach
  salt and pepper
  a few chopped herbs, fresh thyme and parsley

  Beurre Blanc

  8 fl oz (225 ml) chicken stock
  8 fl oz (225 ml) white wine
  4 oz (125 g) softened butter
  4 tablespoons thick cream
  salt and pepper

Set oven at 350°F (280°C, Gas 4). First make the timbales: beat the eggs and cream together, adding the herbs and the vegetable purée and season. Spoon the mixture into 8 buttered individual moulds and bake in a bain-marie for 25 minutes. To make the sauce, reduce the stock and wine by half and then gently beat in the butter, bit by bit. When the sauce is thick, stir in the cream and season to taste.

Test the timbales are firm with your finger and proceed to turn them out on to individual warm plates. Decorate with the warm vegetables and serve immediately.

Warm Duck and Pear Salad in Raspberry Vinaigrette

Serves four

An unusual combination of fruit and game, arranged in an artistic way, can make a delightful starter, or a summer main course for two.

1 × 2 lb (900 g) wild duck
oil and crushed garlic
salt and pepper
watercress and lettuce, trimmed and clean
2 ripe, unblemished pears

Raspberry Vinaigrette

1 dessertspoon very finely chopped parsley
1 dessertspoon very finely chopped shallots
¼ cup raspberry vinegar or raspberry juice and vinegar
1 dessertspoon very finely chopped walnuts
1 cup sunflower oil
salt and pepper

Set oven at 400°F (200°C, Gas 6). Whisk all the ingredients together to make the vinaigrette. Rub the skin of the duck with the oil and crushed garlic and roast for 1 hour or until just pink. Carve the meat into small, neat slices and keep warm.

Prepare the salads and arrange on each plate. Peel and slice the pears and arrange them on top of the salads with the slices of duck. Pour over the vinaigrette and decorate with a few leaves of watercress. Serve immediately.

Asparagus au Gratin

Serves four

This would make a delicious light lunch dish or, alternatively, a rather special vegetable to accompany a simple roast chicken.

    15 oz (425 g) canned asparagus *or*
    1 lb (450 g) fresh asparagus
    1 oz (25 g) butter
    3 tablespoons onion, chopped
    2 × 14 oz (397 g) canned chopped tomatoes
    oregano and thyme
    salt and pepper
    4 tablespoons freshly grated cheddar cheese
    4 tablespoons fine breadcrumbs
    1 dessertspoon freshly grated parmesan

Set oven at 350°F (180°C, Gas 4). Trim the asparagus. Melt the butter in a saucepan and cook the onion until transparent. Stir in the tomatoes and herbs and simmer for 2 – 3 minutes. Season to taste.

Poach the asparagus in boiling water and drain. Arrange them in an oven-proof dish and cover with the tomato sauce. Sprinkle with the parmesan and cheddar cheese and breadcrumbs. Dot with butter and bake for 15 minutes or until the top is golden brown.

For 6 people: increase the quantity of asparagus but keep to the remaining quantitities.

Fennel, Almond and Gruyère Bake

Serves six

This also would make rather a good lunch dish with a crisp mixed salad.

6 very small fennel, trimmed
1 pint (600 ml) single cream
1 large egg
2 oz (50 g) grated gruyère
2 oz (50 g) grated parmesan
salt and pepper
2 oz (50 g) flaked almonds

Set oven at 350°F (180°C, Gas 4). Cook the fennel for 20 minutes in boiling salted water. Drain and arrange in a small oven-proof dish. Whisk together the cream, egg, half of the gruyère and parmesan. Season and pour the mixture over the fennel and sprinkle with the remaining cheeses and the flaked almonds.

Bake for 30 – 40 minutes until the fennel is tender, the custard is set and the nuts are golden brown.

Smoked Salmon and Hazelnut Rolls

Serves four

To make delicious cocktail party or buffet nibbles, simply cut the salmon rolls into much smaller pieces and place on small squares of thin, buttered brown bread.

4 large thin slices smoked salmon
8 oz (225 g) solid cream cheese
2 oz (50 g) hazelnuts, crushed and roasted
2 oz (50 g) double cream
fresh black pepper
twists of lemon and watercress to decorate

Thin brown bread and butter

Beat the cream with a wooden spoon and mix in the cream and hazelnuts. Season to taste. Spoon the mixture on to the slices of salmon and roll up into a big sausage. Trim the edges and cut in half. Sprinkle lightly with cayenne and serve on plates decorated with twists of lemon and fresh watercress or parsley.

Spinach and Crab Terrine
in Tomato Vinaigrette

Serves twelve-fourteen

This terrine fills one large or two small terrine tins.

2 lb (900 g) fresh or frozen leaf
    spinach
1 oz (25 g) aspic jelly powder
juice of half a lemon
2 cups of fresh, frozen or tinned
    crab
2 oz (50 g) butter
1 oz (25 g) flour
1½ cups of milk
a few drops of tabasco
2 teaspoons Worcestershire
    sauce

1 cup of Crème Fraîche or
    Jockey cream cheese
½ oz (11 g) gelatine dissolved in
    hot water
salt and pepper

Tomato Vinaigrette

½ pint (300 ml) tomato juice
¼ pint (150 ml) olive oil
juice of 1 lemon
2 teaspoons Dijon mustard
salt and pepper

First grease the tin with a little butter. Make the vinaigrette in the liquidizer by combining all the ingredients together for a few seconds. Leave the sauce to chill in the refrigerator.

Wash the spinach and remove the stalks. Boil in salted water for 5 minutes. Drain the spinach and chop roughly. Dissolve the aspic in ¾ pint (400 ml) boiled water. Add the lemon juice and leave to cool. Pour some aspic over the base and sides of the terrine tin and chill until set. Spoon in half the spinach and pour half the aspic over it. Chill to set. If you are using 2 terrine tins divide the spinach and aspic equally between them.

Now make the crab filling by melting the butter and stirring in the flour. Gradually stir in the milk and then the crab. Cook the mixture until the sauce boils and then season to taste. Flavour with tabasco and Worcestershire sauce. Cool the mixture slightly before adding the

Mousse 2

8 oz (225 g) fresh salmon steak
1 oz (25 g) butter
1 oz (25 g) cream cheese
2 tablespoons double cream
1 tablespoon medium sherry
1 – 2 drops carmine colouring
½ oz (11 g) gelatine dissolved in water

Béchamel Sauce

¾ cup of hot milk
bayleaf
mace
8 peppercorns
salt
1 sliced onion
1 oz (25 g) butter
1 oz (25 g) flour

Warm the milk with the first five ingredients. Strain the milk before making the Béchamel sauce.

Poach the salmon in a little white wine, water and lemon juice and black pepper. Remove skin and bones and flake the fish. Make the Béchamel sauce and stir in the salmon, butter, sherry, cream, cream cheese and taste for seasoning. Add carmine and stir in the gelatine.

Cool the mixture and then spoon the mousse into the mould over the cucumber mousse. Now cover the salmon mousse with the remaining cucumber mousse. Smooth over and chill for a few hours. Turn out and decorate.

Sesame Seed Toasts

Allow three pieces of toast per person

These toasts are delicious with any soup or mousse.

pita bread
butter
sesame seeds

Carefully slice through each pita bread. Separate the 2 halves and butter them. Sprinkle with sesame seeds and cut into quarters or eights depending on the size of the pita bread.

Arrange under the grill and bake under medium heat until brown and crispy. Keep them in a warm oven until needed.

Seafood Terrine

Serves six – eight

Terrines seem to be very trendy at the moment. They are a bit of a fiddle, but this one is well worth the effort.

8 oz (225 g) butter, to line and seal the mould
12 king prawns, shells removed
2 oz (50 g) butter
½ medium onion, finely chopped
12 scallops
8 oz (225 g) white fish fillets
1 tablespoon chopped parsley
1 clove garlic peeled and crushed
salt and pepper
a few drops tabasco
1 tablespoon cognac, warmed
½ cup double cream, whipped
juice of half a lemon
2 oz (50 g) butter, softened

Line the inside of a loaf tin mould with soft butter, make sure it is quite thick. Leave enough to cover the finished terrine. Chill the mould until the butter has set. Set aside 3 prawns. Melt 2 oz (50 g) butter in a frying pan and cook the chopped onion slowly until soft, add the scallops and fish, cook for a few minutes. Stir in the garlic, parsley, salt and pepper, lemon juice and tabasco. Flame in cognac. Toss the prawns in the pan and simmer for a minute or two. Adjust seasoning.

Cool the mixture, drain and reserve the juices from the pan. Process the fish and shellfish in a electric mixer with 2 oz (50 g) softened butter and fold in the cream. Put half the pâté in the mould. Lay the three prawns across the centre of the terrine. Place remaining pâté in the mould and seal top with more softened butter.

Chill for 8 hours before serving with hot toast.

Salmon Tartare and Cucumber Salad

Serves four

Like steak tartare this recipe is made from raw flesh. It is marinated for 24 hours and then served with a delicious combination of dill and cucumber. I have suggested that you can use caviar or lumpfish to decorate, but it is not listed in the ingredients.

Fresh parsley for decoration
13 oz (350 g) fresh salmon fillets

Marinade

2 oz (50 g) castor sugar
2 oz (50 g) salt
zest of half a lemon
black pepper
1 teaspoon dill weed

Cucumber Salad

½ cucumber, peeled and cut
    into matchsticks
½ tablespoon wine vinegar
½ tablespoon castor sugar
black pepper
chopped dill

4 dessertspoons of crème fraîche
black pepper and cayenne

Remove all the bones from the salmon with a pair of tweezers and arrange 4 fillets of salmon in a china dish. Make the marinade. Combine all the ingredients together in a small bowl and spoon over the salmon fillets. Leave the salmon to marinate for 24 hours, turning the fish around occasionally.

Wash the marinade off the salmon in cold water and pat dry with a clean cloth. Remove the flesh from the skin and process in the magimix for a few seconds until minced. Arrange a large spoonful of the salmon in the centre of each plate. Place a spoonful of the crème fraîche to one side of the salmon tartare. Sprinkle with a little cayenne, or for a special occasion some caviar.

Mix all the ingredients for the cucumber salad and arrange decoratively around the other side of the salmon. Sprinkle a little freshly chopped parsley and freshly ground black pepper over the salmon tartare and keep chilled until served.

Smoked Trout Pâté

Serves eight

2 whole smoked trout
8 oz (226 g) Cottage Cheese
3 tablespoons double cream
salt and pepper
2 teaspoons horseradish sauce
lemon juice to taste

1 lemon and some parsley to decorate

Carefully remove all the bones and skin from the fish. Flake the fish into a magimix and add all the remaining ingredients. Mix thoroughly and transfer the smooth pâté to a dish. Decorate the centre of the pâté with a tiny sprig of parsley and two small slices of lemon.

Tunafish Soufflé

Serves four

7 oz (198 g) flaked tunafish
2 tablespoons grated parmesan
1½ oz (37 g) butter
1½ oz (37 g) flour
½ pint (300 ml) milk
3 tablespoons double cream
cayenne, salt and pepper
4 egg yolks
5 egg whites
extra parmesan for dusting

Set oven at 375°F (190°C, Gas 5). Prepare the soufflé dish. Grease the 2 pint (1200 ml) soufflé dish with butter and half the parmesan, wrap a band of greaseproof paper around the sides of the dish and secure with string.

Melt the butter in a large pan and stir in the flour, gradually pour in the milk and stir until boiling. Draw the pan aside and stir in the cream and tunafish, seasoning and remaining parmesan cheese. Beat in the egg yolks. Whisk the egg whites stiffly, cut and fold 1 large spoonful into the mixture and then fold in the rest. Dust the soufflé with a sprinkling of parmesan and bake for 25 – 30 minutes. Serve immediately.

Smoked Trout Ramekins

Serves eight – ten

4 whole smoked trout
2 lb (900 g) fresh tomatoes, skin and seeds removed
½ pint (300 ml) double cream
1 oz (25 g) butter
4 oz (125 g) grated gruyère
salt and freshly ground black pepper

Set oven at 400°F (200°C, Gas 6). Remove the skin and flake the fish. Chop the tomatoes. Butter the ramekins and spoon half the tomatoes into them and cover with a layer of smoked trout. Season and repeat the layers. Pour the cream over the fish, sprinkle cheese over the top and dot with butter.

Place them in the oven for 10 – 15 minutes until golden and bubbling.

Danish Lumpfish Spaghetti

Serves four

This is wonderfully quick and easy, ideal if you have no time to prepare anything in advance.

1 × 2 oz (60 g) jar of Danish Black Lumpfish or caviar
8 oz (225 g) spaghetti or tagliatelle
2 oz (50 g) unsalted butter
fresh black pepper
2 teaspoons freshly grated parmesan
1 egg yolk
4 tablespoons double cream

Place the pasta in salted boiling water until cooked *al dente*! Drain the spaghetti and toss in butter over low heat, swiftly followed by the cream, pepper, parmesan and egg yolk preferably beaten together first.

Serve the pasta on warmed plates and sprinkle the lumpfish all over. Serve at once.

Fresh Haddock Mousseline
in Basil Sauce

Serves six – eight

Use this basic recipe with other fish and shellfish. You can vary the
mousseline to scallops, salmon, sole, prawns or lobster. They are very
quick and easy to make in a magimix.

Use 6 – 8 Ramekins or Dariol moulds.

1 lb (450 g) fresh haddock
salt and pepper
1 whole egg
1 egg white
¾ pint (450 ml) double cream
butter
6 – 8 prawns in their shells, cooked

Basil Sauce

8 fl oz (225 ml) fish stock (or 1 fish stock cube)
½ onion very finely chopped
8 fl oz (225 ml) white wine
twig of fresh thyme
fresh basil finely chopped
2 tomatoes, skins and seeds removed, and finely chopped
2 tablespoons very thick cream
6 oz (175 g) unsalted butter, in little bits

Set oven at 350°F (180°C, Gas 4). Make the mousselines first. Remove all the bones and skin from the fish. Purée the fish in the food processor until very smooth. Season with salt and pepper. Add the whole egg and egg white. Blend for a further minute. Chill the mixture in the bowl of the food processor for 30 minutes in the refrigerator. Briefly blend the cream into the mixture and then return to the refrigerator for a further hour.

Grease 6 – 8 moulds with butter and line with circles of greaseproof paper. Fill each mould with the fish mixture and bake in a bain-marie for 10 minutes until just set. Make the sauce whilst the mousselines are cooking. Keep the mousselines warm while you finish making the sauce.

Combine the fish stock, onion, wine and thyme and reduce by half over a very high heat. This usually takes about 10 – 15 minutes.

Remove the bouillon from the heat and stir in the tomatoes and basil. Gradually beat in the little bits of butter and return to a very low heat; do not boil the sauce. The sauce should be smooth and glossy. Stir in the cream over the heat and make the sauce thick.

Turn the moulds on to warm plates and pour the sauce around the mousselines. Decorate each mousseline with a prawn and serve immediately.

Wine with Fish

Dry white wines are best with fish – whether it is a plain sole, or something in a rich sauce. The flavours will complement each other whereas red wines tend to taste metallic.

Burgundy produces the finest white wine in the world. Wonderful rich 'fat' wines at the top end, stylish and representative of the Chardonnay grape at the more basic level. I could drink this area's produce for ever!

However, most dry white wines of the world will do, so it is up to your palate and pocket – the world, as they say, is your oyster!

Over £10

CORTON CHARLEMAGNE	Burgundy, Côtes de Beaune	Fat, rich buttery flavour – real Chardonnay – with an enormous sometimes smokey finish.
HERMITAGE BLANC	Northern Rhône	Big, earth flavour. Powerful dry wine.

£5 – £10

MEURSAULT	Burgundy, Côtes de Beaune	Tangy, green sharp flavour when young.
POUILLY FUMÉ	Loire	Smokey, gooseberry nose, full rich mouthful of fruit.

Under £5

MUSCADET DE SÈVRE ET MAINE SUR LIE	Loire	The standard Muscadet is a good wine – 'sur lie' has a richer fuller style.
BULGARIAN CHARDONNAY	Bulgaria	This grape variety crops up again – this time a simple style which is very good value for money.

Plaice and Smoked Salmon Paupiettes

Serves eight

8 fresh prawns in their shells, cooked
8 × 3.5 oz (100 g) fillet plaice, skins removed
5 oz (150 g) inexpensive smoked salmon, finely sliced
3 oz (75 g) butter
2 oz (50 g) flour
3 small wineglasses of fish stock
2 small wineglasses of sparkling wine
3 tablespoons double cream
salt and pepper and a little tarragon
finely chopped parsley
butter

Set oven at 375°F (190°C, Gas 5). Roll the smoked salmon up inside the plaice fillets and lay them in a buttered gratin dish.

Make the sauce: melt the butter and make a roux with the flour, stock and sparkling wine. When you have achieved a smooth sauce, stir in the cream and season to taste. Only use a very little tarragon if it is dried as the flavour is so much stronger.

Pour the sauce over the fish and bake for 15 minutes. Decorate with the prawns and a little parsley.

Monkfish aux Herbes Fines

Serves four – six

1½ lb (700 g) monkfish
2 tablespoons olive oil
2 onions finely sliced
3 tablespoons brandy
1 clove garlic, crushed
salt and pepper
¾ lb (350 g) tomatoes, skinned, seeds removed and chopped
1 wineglass white wine
chopped chives
tarragon, basil, parsley
1 tablespoon tomato paste

Heat the oil, add the onions and cook until just turning colour. Stir in the garlic, tomatoes and the paste, seasoning, brandy, and herbs. Simmer for 3 – 4 minutes and add the wine. Simmer for a minute or so longer. Finally, add the monkfish, and shake the pan continuously over high heat until the fish is cooked.

Serve on a bed of hot savoury rice.

Red Mullet Niçoise

Serves four

4 red mullet
4 tablespoons olive oil
2 cloves garlic finely crushed
2 teaspoons tomato paste
2 wine glasses white wine
oregano and thyme
½ teaspoon paprika pepper
salt and pepper
4 oz (125 g) black olives
8 fresh tomatoes, skinned, seeded and quartered
1 onion, very finely sliced

Set the oven at 350°F (180°C, Gas 4). Heat the onion in a small pan with the oil and paprika and cook gently. Stir in the garlic and herbs. Simmer them with the tomatoes, tomato paste and olives. Stir in the wine, season and simmer.

Wash the fish and remove the gills, dry and place in an oven-proof dish. Pour over the tomato sauce, cover with foil and bake for 20 minutes.

This is also delicious cold.

Trout in Garlic

This is an idea from a delightful restaurant that we went to in San Remo, Italy. They used a delicious Mediterranean fish for which I have substituted the more available trout!

For each trout use the following ingredients:

1 – 2 large cloves fresh garlic, crushed
1 tablespoon chopped parsley
salt and pepper
lemon juice
butter

Wash and dry the trout and lay in an oven-proof dish, sprinkle with lemon juice, butter, garlic and parsley.

Bake for 20 minutes, spooning the juices over from time to time. Serve with new potatoes and a salad.

Sole with Scallops in Chervil Sauce

Serves four

2 whole sole, skinned and filleted into 8 pieces
8 small scallops
2 tablespoons fresh chervil
8fl oz (225 ml) double cream
4 oz (125 g) unsalted butter
5 fl oz (150 ml) sparkling wine or champagne
5 fl oz (150 ml) fish stock (½ stock cube is fine)
juice of half a lemon
black pepper

Set oven at 375°F (190°C, Gas 5). Beat the fish fillets with a rolling pin under grease-proof paper and then roll them around each scallop. Arrange them in a well buttered (use 1 oz (25 g) of the 4 oz (125 g)) dish. Sprinkle with lemon juice, black pepper, fish stock and wine. Cook for about 12 minutes.

Remove the fish on to another plate and keep warm while you make the sauce. Reduce the fish liquor for 10 minutes in a saucepan and then remove it from the heat. Gradually beat in the butter until the sauce is thick, return to low heat, do not boil, and stir in the cream and chervil. Adjust the seasoning and serve immediately. Place 2 fillets of fish on each warmed plate and pour the sauce around the fish.

Salmon in Whisky and Mushroom Sauce

Serves four

I had never used whisky with fish before this recipe. Surprisingly, it makes a very subtle and smooth sauce.

4 × 5 oz (150 g) fresh salmon steaks
2 × 2 oz (50 g) butter in small bits
2 oz (50 ml) whisky
8 oz (225 ml) double cream
juice of half a lemon
6 oz (175 g) button mushrooms, sliced
salt and pepper
2 teaspoons chopped parsley

Melt 2 oz (50 g) butter and cook the salmon over low heat for 5 minutes in a large frying pan. Pour over the lemon juice and season, cook for another five minutes but only turn the salmon over once. Remove the steaks and keep warm. Sauté the mushrooms in the same pan, flame the whisky and stir in the cream. Reduce slightly, remove from the heat and shake in the remaining butter. Do not reboil. Arrange the salmon, pour over the sauce and decorate with parsley.

Seafood Barbecue Parties

Seafood always tastes absolutely marvellous when cooked and eaten outside in the relaxed atmosphere of a barbecue. Pay special attention to your table decoration: lots of flowers and candles, old paraffin lamps and floodlights all combine to give you a wonderful evening.

The Choice of Fish

Richer, more oily fish are the best to use because they keep their shape better during cooking and do not flake too easily. The most suitable and available fish are trout, red mullet, sardines or salmon, halibut and turbot. You can also use monkfish, scallops and prawns to make delicious kebabs.

Barbecuing Guidelines

Use smaller whole fish and fish steaks so that they do not get overcooked on the outside whilst being underdone near the bone.

Ensure that the fish is washed and de-scaled. Slash the flesh of a whole fish 2 or 3 times on each side according to size. The fish can then be marinated. Use ¼ pint olive oil with 3 tablespoons red wine vinegar, 1 small onion sliced, 1 clove garlic, crushed, salt and pepper and lots of fresh or dried herbs. Alternatively, use chilies and cayenne instead of herbs to make a spicy marinade. Marinate for a couple of hours.

To make sure the fish holds its shape, cook wrapped in a clean small mesh chicken wire. Cook over the ashy glow of a charcoal fire that has been tended for an hour or so. Whole fish should cook for about 10 minutes on each side. Fish steaks probably only 5 minutes. To test if a whole fish is cooked make sure that the thick flesh immediately behind the head is firm.

Brush the fish with the marinade during cooking. The skin should become deliciously crispy. Serve with flavoured butters or mayonnaise based sauces, crispy french bread and green salads.

Prawn and Bacon Kebabs with Anchovy Mayonnaise

You can make your kebabs as long or as short as you like. You can also use vegetables such as cherry tomatoes and button mushrooms or blanched peppers and onions. You can marinate the shellfish first.

For example use: 2 prawns, wrapped in bacon
2 cubes monkfish, wrapped in bacon
2 small scallops, wrapped in bacon – per person.

It is very important to wrap the shellfish in bacon to keep it moist. Cook over the barbecue until the bacon is crispy. Serve with anchovy mayonnaise and fresh french bread.

Anchovy Mayonnaise

double cream
Hellmans mayonnaise
anchovy paste or essence
freshly ground black pepper
sprinkle of cayenne
2 oz (50 g) anchovy fillets in oil
milk

Soak the anchovies for 30 minutes in milk. Rinse well and pat dry on paper towels. Finely chop the anchovies and combine with all the remaining ingredients. The sauce should be of pouring consistency.

Seafood Barbecue

Halibut with Chinese Ginger Sauce

Turbot and salmon steaks are also delicious with this sauce.

Fresh Halibut

Chinese Ginger Sauce
2 very finely chopped shallots
juice of 1 lemon
salt and freshly ground black pepper
6 tablespoons soy sauce
2 tablespoons clear honey
1″ cube finely grated fresh ginger root
melted butter for fish

Combine all the sauce ingredients in a saucepan and boil for 2 – 3 minutes. Make this sauce as sweet or tangy as you like. Brush the fish with the melted butter and then brush with a little sauce. Keep spooning the sauce over the fish during cooking time. Keep the sauce warm over the fire. Spoon a little sauce over each fish steak and serve immediately.

Red Mullet Niçoise

Follow the recipe on page 56. Instead of putting the fish in the oven-proof dish, wrap each mullet in foil with the sauce inside and cook over the barbecue until the flesh is firm.

Salmon with Sorrel and Watercress Butter

Serves eight

Use this butter for any grilled fish, lamb chops or steak. It is also excellent with barbecued lobster or chicken.

melted butter
8 salmon steaks

Sorrell and Watercress Butter

8 oz (225 g) unsalted butter, softened
a handful of fresh sorrel, stalks removed
1 bunch watercress, stalks removed
1 handful of fresh parsley, stalks removed
a few fresh tarragon leaves
salt and pepper

Combine all the ingredients together in a magimix. Spoon the butter on-to the foil in a long sausage shape, wrap up and chill. Cut into pats and freeze if you wish to. Serve one pat per person, placed on the salmon steak immediately after cooking.

To cook the salmon brush with melted butter or a herb marinade, recipe on page 44 and cook until the flesh is firm.

Wine with Poultry and Game

Depending on how your game is 'hung', either a red wine or a full white wine will do. Red wine usually stands up to richer flavours. Simply prepared poultry benefits from a lighter white wine – something like duck, however, can suit both.

White Wines – Over £10

RIESLING LES ECAILLERS d'ALSACE. BEYER

Fine rich dry wine from North East France.

£5 – £10

CHARDONNAY di MEZZOCORONA 1984. BOLLINI Trentino

An Italian version of the grape used for white Burgundy, with a softer style.

SANCERRE Loire

Near to Pouilly Fumé on the Loire, but a sharper, tangier flavour.

Under £5

MÂCON VILLAGES

South of Burgundy lies the 'Mâconnais'. Cheaper than Burgundy, but a good Chardonnay style.

CORVO WHITE

A rich, full but still light wine from Sicily.

Red Wines – Over £10

BAROLO Piedmont, Northern Italy

Old vintages (1958, 1967) are quite amazing. Thick rich tarry flavours which soften into scented violets.

£5 – £10

HERMITAGE

A big rich wine from the Rhône which needs age and a long time to breathe.

ROBERT MONDAVI'S PINOT NOIR Napa Valley

Californian Burgundy! Still a top producer's wine, with age softening to a rich mellow 'hot' flavour of Pinot.

Under £5

CÔTES DU VENTOUX

Lighter southern style of Rhône. Very good value for everyday drinking.

LISTEL GRIS DE GRIS Southern France

A wonderful dry rose from the Camargue. Very good price for a very well made wine.

Chicken in Peanut Sauce

Serves six

6 chicken portions dusted with flour
½ lb (227 g) jar smooth peanut butter
1 teaspoon turmeric
1 teaspoon curry powder
1 teaspoon ground ginger
½ teaspoon crushed cardamom
ground black pepper
1 large onion, finely chopped
3 oz (75 g) butter
1 pint (600 ml) chicken stock

Sauté the onion with all the spices and seasoning in the butter in a thick bottomed casserole for 5 minutes. Then sauté the chicken pieces. When they are well browned, cover them with peanut butter and gradually stir in the stock. Simmer for 20 minutes on a low heat until the chicken is cooked.

Serve with Savoury Rice made from chicken stock and poppadums.

Chicken and Sweetcorn Casserole

Serves four – six

This is ideal for a cheap and cheerful dinner party, with baked potatoes and a green salad.

3½ lb (1600 g) fresh chicken, cut into 8 pieces
2 tablespoons bacon fat
1 onion chopped
1 pint strong chicken stock
½ lb (225 g) smoked back bacon
1 sprig of fresh thyme
2 dessertspoons cornflour in a little water
5 fl oz (150 ml) double cream
12 oz (340 g) tin golden sweetcorn
fresh lemon juice to taste
2 tablespoons finely chopped parsley
2 tablespoons finely chopped chives

Set oven at 400°F (200°C, gas 6). Sauté the chicken and thyme in a casserole in the bacon fat, add the onion and bacon and cook for 5 minutes before pouring the stock over. Bake the chicken for 40 minutes in the oven or until tender.

Remove the chicken from the oven onto low heat and stir in the cornflour to thicken. Add the sweetcorn and cream, season to taste with lemon juices, salt and pepper. Just before serving, sprinkle with the parsley and chives.

Chicken in Watercress Sauce

Serves six

6 chicken breasts
1 oz (25 g) butter
14 fl oz (400 ml) chicken stock
10 fl oz (300 ml) thick cream
2 large egg yolks
salt and pepper
1 bunch watercress trimmed and washed
1 teaspoon of lemon juice
¼ pint (150 ml) white wine
3 dessertspoons, very finely chopped onions
extra watercress for decoration

Sauté the chicken in butter with the onion. Pour over the wine and stock and cook over medium heat for about 20 – 25 minutes. Combine the cream and egg yolks in a cup.

Remove the chicken from the pan and keep warm. Purée the stock and watercress together, add the lemon juice and seasoning. Finally, add the cream and egg mixture and blend thoroughly.

Spoon the sauce over the chicken and decorate with watercress.

Chicken in Garlic Crisps

Serves six

Lucy and I used this recipe in Merribel where we were cooking for the summer. It was always very popular with all the guests.

6 chicken breasts, skins removed
2 family sized packets salted crisps, approximately 5 oz (150 g)
3 tablespoons chopped parsley
3 cloves garlic, crushed
3 tablespoons softened butter
fresh black pepper

Set oven at 375°F (190°C, Gas 4). Crush the crisps. Mix the ingredients together and spread the mixture over the chicken breasts. Cook the chicken in a roasting tin for 40 minutes and serve hot with a delicious crispy salad.

Poultry and Game!

Chicken in Pineapple Sauce and Lemon Rice

Serves twenty four. Halve the quantity for twelve

This is ideal for large buffets, and you can display the pineapple tops in the centre of the dish. It is very light and refreshing.

4 chickens, roasted
2 fresh pineapples, peeled and finely chopped
2 packets watercress
1 pint (600 ml) whipped cream
14 oz (400 g) mayonnaise
16 oz (450 g) natural set yoghurt

Chop the chickens into manageable pieces and transfer to a large mixing bowl. Stir in the pineapple and fold in the mayonnaise, yoghurt and cream. Season to taste and chill. Serve either on a bed of rice or all mixed up together. Decorate with the watercress.

Lemon Rice

For 2.2 lb (1000 g) rice use the juice and rind of 3 lemons, plenty of salt and pepper. If serving the rice separately, then sprinkle it with fresh chopped parsley.

Sauté Chicken and Courgettes

Serves six

Start cooking this 20 minutes before serving so that it keeps crisy, but fair warning, it does stink the kitchen out!

6 portions of chicken, dipped in seasoned flour
6 – 7 cloves garlic, finely crushed
12 young courgettes, finely sliced
salt and pepper
2 oz (50 g) olive oil
4 tablespoons very finely chopped onion
2 oz (50 g) butter
2 tablespoons chopped parsley

Melt the butter and the oil with the garlic and fry the chicken on all sides so that it is well browned. Sauté the onions with the chicken and at the last minute toss the courgettes into the pan and sauté briefly. Season and sprinkle with parsley and serve with hot crusty bread and a salad.

Smokey Devilled Pheasant

Serves six

2 cooked pheasants, legs must be under-done
7 fl oz (200 ml) bottle smokey BBQ sauce
2 tablespoons Worcestershire sauce
dash of anchovy essence
1.26 lb (570 g) bottle tomato ketchup

Béchamel Sauce

3 oz (75 g) butter
3 oz (75 g) flour
½ pint (300 ml) milk
½ pint (300 ml) single cream
nutmeg, salt and pepper

chopped fresh parsley
chopped crispy bacon

Set oven at 375°F (190°C, Gas 5). Remove the pheasant legs from the carcase and separate the thighs from the drumsticks. Marinate for as long as possible in the BBQ sauce mixed with the other ingredients. Cook the pheasant legs and thighs until they are crispy, baste them as often as possible.

Make the Béchemel sauce and chop up all the remaining pheasant meat and incorporate it into the sauce. Cook for 5 – 10 minutes. Grill the bacon and chop it up.

To assemble: Arrange the pheasant legs and thighs around a large, warm oval or round dish. Spoon the pheasant in white sauce into the middle of the dish and sprinkle over the chopped bacon and parsley.

Pheasant Bonne Femme

Serves six

This is an exceptionally good pheasant dish. If you need to make large quantities you can freeze the pheasant in wine sauce and on the day you need it, thaw the mixture and add the mushrooms, bacon and hollandaise sauce.

2 pheasants
1 tablespoon butter
salt and pepper
3 slices back bacon for each bird
1 wine glass white wine

1 wine glass water
8 oz (225 g) mushrooms wiped
  clean and finely sliced
squeeze lemon juice
1 oz (25 g) butter

White Sauce

2 oz (50 g) butter
2 oz (50 g) flour
½ pint (300 ml) pheasant juices
  from the pan
5 tablespoons cream
salt and pepper

Hollandaise Sauce

4 egg yolks
1 tablespoon lemon juice
6 oz (175 g) boiling butter
fresh black pepper
1 tablespoon of hot water

Set oven at 375°F (190°C, Gas 5). First fill the pan with the wine and the water. Place the pheasants in the pan, smeared in butter, seasoned and wrapped up in bacon. Baste as often as possible. Sauté the mushrooms in butter and lemon juice and set to one side. Make the hollandaise sauce. Boil the butter and gradually pour into an electric blender with the eggs, lemon and seasoning already in. Blend until thick. Leave in the blender until needed. At the last minute thin the sauce with a little hot water.

Make the white sauce with the pheasant juices and cream and season to taste. Keep covered until needed.

Strip the meat off the birds and arrange in an oven-proof gratin dish. Pour over the white sauce and sprinkle over the mushrooms. Cut the bacon into little bits and sprinkle over the mushrooms. Cover the whole dish with the hollandaise sauce and bake in the oven for 20 minutes until hot and bubbling in a higher temperature of 400°F (200°C, Gas 6).

Woodcock on Chestnut Pâté

Serves six

I love the combination of chestnut and game, and this pâté is so easy to make.

6 woodcock, arrange the bird neatly, stick the beak through the wing
15 oz (425 g) tin unsweetened chestnut purée
6 slices toast
nutmeg, salt and pepper, to taste
medium sweet sherry, to taste
3 fl oz (75 ml) double cream
fresh thyme

Set oven at 400°F (200°C, Gas 6). Roast the birds for 15 – 20 minutes depending on your own preference. While you are roasting the birds, prepare the pâté. Mash the chestnut purée with the cream and seasoning. Stir in the sherry and thyme and heat through in a non-stick saucepan. Make the toast and spread the chestnut pâté over each one. Place a woodcock on each piece of toast and serve immediately.

If there are enough juices in the pan, reduce them over high heat for a second or two and stir in a little more sherry and thyme. Season to taste and pour over the woodcock.

Venison and Chestnut Pie

Serves eight

On the few occasions that we are given a haunch of venison, I usually roast it, but these recipes are well worth sacrificing the roast, and it stretches a little venison much further!

2.2 lb (1 kg) venison, cut into cubes
1 lb (450 g) green back bacon
15 oz (425 g) tin unsweetened chestnuts
2 large onions, finely sliced into circles
2 oz (50 g) plain flour
2 oz (50 g) butter
2 tablespoons olive oil
¼ pint (150 ml) medium sherry
beef stock to cover
2 tablespoons Worcestershire sauce
1 tablespoon tomato paste
nutmeg, salt and pepper
½ teaspoon mixed spice
½ teaspoon fresh thyme
brown sugar to taste
1 large packet frozen puff pastry or flaky pastry
1 beaten egg to glaze
extra cornflour

Set oven at 350°F (180°C, Gas 4). Melt the butter with the oil in a big casserole and sauté the venison, onions and bacon until the meat has browned all over. Stir in the flour and tomato paste, all the other seasonings, spices, thyme, brown sugar, stock, sherry and Worcestershire sauce. Blend the ingredients thoroughly, cover and cook for an hour and a half or until tender.

Thicken the casserole with cornflour if necessary and add the chestnuts. Leave to cool slightly. Transfer the venison to a large pie dish and cover with pastry. Glaze the pastry with the beaten egg and decorate with any leftover bits of pastry. Bake for 10 minutes at 400°F (200°C, Gas 6) and then turn the temperature down to 375°F (190°C, Gas 5) and continue to bake for 20 – 25 minutes or until well risen and golden brown.

Venison Shepherd's Pie

Serves six

1¼ lb (550 g) cold roast venison
1 large onion, finely chopped
5 carrots, finely chopped
1 tablespoon chopped celery
1 – 2 cloves garlic, crushed
6 juniper berries, crushed
plenty of fresh thyme
salt and pepper
2 oz (50 g) butter
2 tablespoons oil
left over gravy
½ pint (300 ml) red wine
1 dessertspoon tomato paste
1 tablespoon cornflour
1¾ lb (700 g) potatoes, peeled and quartered
2 oz (50 g) butter
nutmeg, salt and black pepper
cream or milk

Mince the venison. Sauté the vegetables in the oil and butter until soft. Stir in the venison, garlic, juniper berries, thyme, salt and pepper and cook for 3 – 4 minutes. Add the gravy, tomato paste and wine and cook for half an hour. Thicken with cornflour if necessary.

Cook and mash the potatoes. Stir in the butter, cream, seasoning and nutmeg. Transfer the mince to an oven-proof dish and cover with the mashed potatoes. Brown in the oven for 15 – 20 minutes.

Duck in Port and Cranberry Sauce

Serves six

The mousses make the dinner extra smart and every one will be very impressed by the extra effort, although they are very easy to make.

2 duck, if very large, or 3 if you
   are nervous!

Duck Mousses

½ small onion, finely chopped
thyme
2 oz (50 g) butter
4 oz (125 g) sliced mushrooms
8 oz (225 g) duck meat, cut from
   legs
2 tablespoons port
nutmeg, salt and pepper
1 whole egg
2 egg whites
¼ pint (150 ml) double cream,
   whipped

Port and Cranberry Sauce

½ onion, finely chopped
2 oz (50 g) butter
salt and pepper
juice of 2 oranges
¼ pint (150 ml) stock
4 dessertspoons cranberry sauce
1 teaspoon grated fresh ginger
¼ pint (150 ml) port
Cornflower in a little water

Set oven at 400°F (200°C, Gas 6). Roast the ducks with a tiny bit of fat over the breasts for about 1¼ – 1½ hours or until just slightly pink. Keep them warm in foil after you have picked off the 8 oz (225 g) meat from the legs.

To make the mousses: sauté the onion in butter and thyme until transparent, then cook the mushrooms. Mince the duck meat with the whole egg and season. Add the onion and mushrooms with the port to the duck and briefly mince it again. When the mixture is cold, fold in the cream and egg whites and carefully spoon into 6 buttered ramekins. Bake in a bain-marie for 25 minutes.

To make the sauce: sweat the onion in the butter for 10 minutes in a saucepan. Stir in the ginger and cook for a further 5 minutes. Pour in the stock, cranberry sauce, port, seasoning and orange juice, and simmer for a few minutes. Thicken with cornflower and keep warm.

To assemble: carve very fine slices of duck and arrange in a fan shape on each warm plate, turn a mousse onto each plate and pour a spoonful of sauce onto the mousse and a spoonful onto the duck. Arrange your vegetables neatly for a special effect.

'Duck!'

Duck in Two Ginger Sauce

Serves four

Do not boil this sauce for long or else the ingredients will separate.

4 duck breasts
12 slices fresh or tinned peaches
2 tablespoons oil and 1 crushed clove of garlic for roasting
a little butter, unsalted

Two Ginger Sauce

1 small onion, finely chopped
1 oz (25 g) butter
¼ pint (150 ml) ginger wine
½ pint (300 ml) chicken stock
2 teaspoons grated fresh ginger
2 dessertspoons very finely chopped stem ginger
cornflour and water to thicken
salt and pepper

Set oven at 400°F (200°C, Gas 6). Roast the duck breasts in a little garlic and oil until just pink. Sauté the onion briefly in a frying pan in the 1 oz (25 g) butter. Stir in the grated ginger and cook for a further 5 minutes. Pour in the ginger wine and simmer for 2 minutes. Pour in the stock and thicken with cornflour. When the breasts are cooked skim off all the fat and add the duck juices to the sauce. Season. Stir in the chopped stem ginger.

Just before serving, gently reheat the sauce and pour it over each portion of duck.

Quickly sauté the peach slices in some foaming butter to warm through. Arrange them neatly around the duck and serve.

Wine with Meat

Red wines are my love – Claret and Burgundy I think are unsurpassed. Of course there are great red wines from all over the world; – I admit that I am biased. Claret is the safer of the two to buy – a château produces its own wine under its own label year in year out. If you like a style it is easier to follow. It is quite easy to appreciate the different qualities of the various districts – Médoc wines – Pauillac and St. Estèphe especially, are tougher wines with real longevity. St. Emilion, Pommerol and St. Julien are softer, richer and more generous of fruit. It tends to be a balance of soil and grape blend.

Over £10

CHÂTEAU GISCOURS 1976
Margaux

Fat rich wine. Soft nose, smooth blackcurrants – well balanced

CLOS DE LA ROCHE.
DOMAINE DUJAC
Côte de Nuits

This wine is not filtered – leaving natural deposits for the wine to live on. Quite light in style, it has a classic 'farm-yard nose' and strawberry tang.

£5 – £10

CHÂTEAU LA LAGUNE
1980 Ludon

For a relatively young wine, the 1980 vintage is light and drinking well now. A good buy.

HAUTES CÔTES DE NUITS

A lightish wine from the area providing great reds of Burgundy. This sort of wine needs to come from a reputable house – or one you know.

Under £5

HOUSE CLARET

A reputable merchant will always have a good standard wine. Their reputation is too much at risk not to.

MORGON

Big Beaujolais, wines from this village age well, and show that Nouveau Beaujolais is far from the best that the gamay grape can provide.

RIOJA GRAN RESERVA
1976. BERBERANA

– Surprise! Real 'jammy' fruit, vanilla and sweet finish. Rioja at its best.

Traditional British Hams & Gammon

Here are a few helpful hints on choosing and keeping Ham and Gammon. I would like to thank Paxton and Whitfield Ltd for all their help.

Cooked Cured Hams

The most important point to remember is that you should taste the ham in the shop before you buy it. It's far too expensive to make a mistake.

Choosing Cooked Hams

Here are three hams that Paxton & Whitfield have in their shop; all of which I thoroughly recommend.

The Wiltshire Gammon should be fleshy and bright pink in colour. It is the most moist of all the hams and has the mildest flavour.

The York Ham should also be fleshy and robust with a good pink colour. This ham has more flavour and is generally the most popular.

The Bradenham Ham has a darker flesh and has a much stronger flavour; usually preferred by men, so I am told!

When you buy a cooked ham you must be very careful to check the following points:

1) It must not be salty
2) The ham must look fresh; if it is dry or tired looking it is no good.
3) The fat should be clearly marbled and not rancid.
4) The breadcrumbs should be fresh and colourful; if they are at all mouldy it is because the ham had not been properly stored.
5) There should be some fat on the ham, but not too much otherwise you are paying for the fat and not the meat.

'Gammoned!'

A very old fashioned way of testing that the ham is fresh, according to Mrs. Beaton, is to insert a skewer into the ham and if it comes out clean and sweet-smelling the meat is good. The flesh nearest the bone goes bad first.

Keeping Ham and Gammon

Only buy as much ham as you need as it does not keep long before it starts to dry out. Carve the ham as you need it, to keep it moist, and always keep the ham covered. You should not keep your Christmas ham for more than 2 weeks, even in a cool place.

Traditional Cured Ham and Gammon

The Gammon is the fleshy back leg of a pig. The ham is the leaner front leg of a pig. So now you know what you are asking for! Cured hams last about 3 – 4 months, but if they are kept in a cool and ventilated room they might last a bit longer. After this period of time they start to lose their flavour.

The ham is cured to preserve it. During the curing process the ham is salted and this is why it must be soaked before cooking. The ham is also smoked; it is hung in a smokehouse over oak or other wood chippings for a specified amount of time according to the flavour required. If a ham is being sold as smoked ham it has been through this process and has a more distinctive smoked flavour. The ham is cooked and sold in shops, either whole or sliced in packets.

Ham is a very old-fashioned commodity. I know how easy it is to buy it already sliced in packets, but this type of ham tends to be full of water and lacks flavour and texture. So it really is worth buying a ham or gammon and cooking it yourself.

I have included a delicious recipe for ham and watercress mousse, a superb Ham and Banana recipe and various other recipes using ham including basic instructions for cooking a whole ham.

Sugar Glazed Ham or Gammon

A heavily salted ham needs 24 hours soaking before boiling. Bring the ham to the boil in fresh water, simmer for 20 minutes and then replace with clean water and a bottle of cider, together with black peppercorns, parsley stalks, a stick of celery and a couple of carrots. Simmer for half the cooking time. I usually allow 25 minutes per pound plus 25 minutes extra for the total cooking time. Roast the joint at 325°F (170°C, Gas 3) for the remaining time. Baste the joint three times whilst cooking.

This quantity is adequate for a 10 – 12 lb joint.

6 oz (175 g) soft dark-brown sugar
6 tablespoons clear honey
2 tablespoons Dijon mustard
Whole cloves

Cut the rind from the cooked ham, score the fat in a criss-cross pattern, cover with mustard and stud with cloves. Cover the base of the tin with a little stock. Spoon over the sugar and honey and roast. Make the sauce with the left over pan juices and plenty of fresh orange juice and seasoning, thicken with cornflour and serve the sauce separately. For a dinner party, add a little Grand-Marnier to the sauce.

Ham and Banana Paupiettes

Serves four

A delicious and unusual combination. This quantity would serve 8 as a starter or savoury.

8 bananas
8 large slices smoked cooked ham
2 oz (50 g) grated Gruyère
2 oz (50 g) grated Emmenthal
2 oz (50 g) butter
½ pint (300 ml) double cream
paprika, salt and pepper

Set oven at 400°F (200°C, Gas 6). Grease a gratin dish with half the butter. Peel the bananas, cut in half, and dust with salt, pepper and paprika. Roll each banana in the ham and trim the edges.

Put the paupiettes in the gratin dish and sprinkle over the cheese and dot with the remaining butter. Pour over the cream and sprinkle with a little paprika and black pepper. Bake the paupiettes for 20 minutes, until golden and bubbling.

Fillet Steak with
Hazelnut Hollandaise Sauce

Serves four

You can make the hazelnut sauce well in advance and gently reheat it,
in a bain-marie, as you cook the steaks.

    1 oz (25 g) butter
    2 teaspoons oil
    4 × 6 oz (175 g) fillet steaks, trimmed
    2 × 2 oz (50 g) packets hazelnuts
    6 oz (175 g) unsalted butter
    4 large egg yolks
    4 teaspoons lemon juice
    black pepper
    garnish of watercress

Roast the hazelnuts until pale brown and rub off the skins, crush them
in a magimix and keep them to one side. Put the egg yolks, lemon juice,
black pepper in the magimix. Give it a brief whizz.

Sauté the steaks in 1 oz butter and oil in a frying pan and keep warm
while the you make the sauce. Boil the butter and slowly pour into the
magimix with the machine running. Stir in the hazelnuts.

Thinly slice the fillet steak and arrange it in a semi-circle around the
centre of the plate. Spoon the sauce around the steak. Decorate with
watercress and serve vegetables separately or arrange the vegetables
neatly with the steak.

Baked Beef and Mozzarella

Serves eight – ten

For 4 – 5 people, halve the ingredients except the cheese topping as you will need the same amount to cover your gratin dish.

3 – 4 large onions, sliced
2.2 lb (1 kg) lean chuck steak
1½ oz (40 g) seasoned flour
5 tablespoons olive oil
1 teaspoon each of ground cinnamon, cumin and cloves
4 tablespoons tomato purée
7 fl oz (200 ml) beef stock
salt and pepper
fresh thyme
cornflour to thicken if needed
1½ lb (575 g) chopped tomatoes
4 cloves crushed garlic
½ pint (300 ml) single cream
1 large egg
2 oz (50 g) cheddar cheese, grated
2 oz (50 g) mozzarella cheese, grated
2 oz (50 g) flaked almonds

Set oven at 350°F (180°C, Gas 4). Cut the meat into 1″ (25 cm) cubes. Sauté the onions in the oil with all the spices and garlic in a large thick casserole dish. Toss the meat in the seasoned flour and sauté in the casserole with the onions. When it is browned all over, stir in the tomato purée, chopped thyme and tomatoes, seasoning and stock.

Simmer in the oven for 1½ hours or until tender. The sauce should be very solid; if it is not, thicken it with some cornflower.

Transfer the meat to a large gratin dish. Whisk the cream, cheeses, egg and seasoning together and pour over the meat. Sprinkle with almonds and bake for 40 minutes until golden and bubbling.

Beef and Lamb!

Lamb in Armagnac Sauce

Serves eight

2 oz (50 g) butter
1 teaspoon fresh thyme
20 fl oz (600 ml) chicken or lamb stock
4½ lb (2 kg) loin lamb, boned and outside skin removed
¼ lb (125 g) chicken livers, cleaned and chopped
¼ lb (125 g) ham chopped
¼ lb (125 g) chopped mushrooms
1 spanish onion chopped
¼ lb (125 g) lambs kidneys chopped
1 fl oz (25 ml) oil and half teaspoon of thyme
1 beaten egg in 2 tablespoons single cream
¼ lb (125 g) breadcrumbs
2 tablespoons medium dry sherry
seasoning
4 fl oz (125 ml) Armagnac
10 fl oz (300 ml) cream for the sauce
2 tablespoons cornflour in water or stock

Set oven at 400°F (200°C, Gas 6). Sauté the onion in butter with 1 teaspoon fresh thyme until transparent, add the chopped livers, ham, mushrooms, and kidneys and cook for a few minutes. Stir in the sherry and seasoning. Remove from the heat and stir in the breadcrumbs, egg and cream.

Pour the stock into a roasting tin. Spread the meat out and fill with the stuffing and tie up securely. Rub the lamb with oil and thyme. Roast until pink for about 1½ hours in the roasting tin. Remove the lamb from the tin and set on a serving dish, and keep warm. Make the sauce with the pan juices, thicken with cornflour, stir in the cream and season to taste. Put the lamb back into the pan and flame with half the Armagnac. Add the remaining Armagnac to the sauce to give a fine strong flavour.

Remove the string from the meat and carve on to a warmed serving plate and pour over the sauce.

Roast Lamb
with Apricot and Amaretto

Serves eight – ten

I made this one as alcoholic as I could. If you do not have any amaretto, you could use Grand Marnier or Orange Curaçao.

4½ lb (2 kg) leg of lamb, boned
2½ oz (65 g) breadcrumbs
5 oz (150 g) chopped dried
    apricots
1 spanish onion, chopped
1 dessertspoon fresh or dried
    celery
1 oz (25 g) butter
1 fl oz (25 ml) oil
salt and pepper and nutmeg
2 fl oz (50 ml) Amaretto di
    Saronno
2 oz (50 g) finely chopped
    walnuts

1 fl oz (25 ml) orange juice
grated rind of half an orange
1 fl oz (25 ml) oil

Sauce

10 fl oz (300 ml) orange juice
4 fl oz (125 ml) Amaretto di
    Saronno
seasoning to taste
1 tablespoon cornflour in water
10 fl oz (300 ml) chicken stock

twists of orange for decoration.

Set oven at 400°F (200°C, Gas 6). Sauté the onion and celery in the butter and oil until soft and transparent. Leave to one side while you make the breadcrumbs.

Chop the apricots and walnuts, cook for 5 minutes with the onion, and season. Mix them into the breadcrumbs with the Amaretto and orange juice and the grated rind of half an orange. Lay the meat on a board and spread over the stuffing. Secure the flesh with skewers and tie up with string. Rub the skin with oil and pour the stock into the pan. Roast for about 1½ hours or until tender.

After the first 1¼ hours, pour over the orange juice and Amaretto and return to the oven. Remove the skewers and place the meat on a warm serving dish. Finally thicken the sauce with the cornflour and season to taste. Arrange twists of orange around the lamb and serve the sauce separately.

Lamb in Paprika Sauce

Serves six

3.3 lb (1½ kg) boned lamb, tightly rolled up and tied with string
1 tablespoon olive oil
1 lb (450 g) tomatoes, peeled and chopped (or use tinned tomatoes)
anchovy paste or essence
2 oz (50 g) unsalted butter
black pepper and paprika
garlic paste
¼ pint (150 ml) double cream
3 tablespoons cognac
a little cornflour in water

Set oven at 400°F (200°C, Gas 6). Rub the lamb with the oil and paprika and roast for 50 minutes. Remove the excess fat from the pan and rub the lamb with a mixture of anchovy paste and garlic paste, black pepper and butter, according to how strong a flavour you desire. Return the meat to the oven surrounded by the chopped tomatoes and continue to cook at 350°F (190°C, Gas 5) for a further 15 minutes.

Carve the lamb on a serving dish and arrange neatly. Keep warm while you make the sauce. Stir the cornflour into the tomatoes and thicken the sauce over a low heat. Spoon over the warmed cognac and flame. Add the cream and adjust the seasoning. Pour the sauce over the meat and serve.

Country Veal Chop Casserole

Serves six

You can adapt this recipe to pork chops and both freeze very well, so does the anchovy bread.

6 large thick veal chops
salt and pepper
nutmeg
3 oz (75 g) butter
1 lb (450 g) bag frozen baby onions
3 oz (75 g) demarara sugar
1 lb (450 g) thick cut back bacon chopped
½ lb (225 g) tiny mushrooms
½ pint (300 ml) beer
cornflour and water to thicken

Sauté the chops and onions in a large casserole dish in the butter and sugar. When nearly caramalized, add the bacon and mushrooms, thoroughly coat all the ingredients and pour the beer over, season to taste and cook gently for ¾ hour until tender. Thicken with cornflour.
    Serve with hot anchovy bread.

Anchovy Bread

1 loaf fresh french bread
4 oz (125 g) butter
1 tin anchovy fillets
black pepper

Slice the bread into 12, but do not slice completely through the bread. Beat the anchovies and pepper with the butter and spread over each slice of bread. Wrap up in foil and bake until hot and crispy.

Veal and Ham Paupiettes

Serves four – six

These are delicious cold and super for a smart picnic.

4 large escalopes veal
4 oz (125 g) very finely chopped ham
4 oz (125 g) very finely chopped onion
salt and black pepper
fresh thyme
2 tablespoons oil
1 oz (25 g) butter
2 oz (50 g) fine breadcrumbs
4 tablespoons marsala or sherry
1 oz (25 g) butter

Place the escalopes in between two sheets of greaseproof paper and beat until very thin. Cut the escalopes in half and trim the edges.

Sauté the onion in the oil, butter and thyme until transparent. Stir in the ham and remove from the heat. Mix in the breadcrumbs and seasoning and fill each piece of veal with the mixture, roll up and tie securely. Heat 1 oz (25 g) butter and thyme and cook veal in a frying pan until brown all over and tender, about 20 minutes.

Untie the threads and arrange them on a warm serving dish. Add marsala with the juices, adjust the seasoning and boil for one minute, scraping all the bits from the pan. Spoon the sauce over the veal and serve.

Your Friendly Butcher

Veal Stroganoff

Serves four

1 lb (450 g) large veal escalopes
10 oz (275 g) mushrooms, finely sliced and washed under cold water
1 onion, very finely sliced
2 oz (50 g) butter
salt, pepper and cayenne pepper
½ pint (300 ml) sour cream
¼ pint (150 ml) white wine
1 – 2 tablespoons brandy

Cut veal into very thin strips. Sauté the onions in the butter and cayenne until transparent. Toss the mushrooms with the onion and then add the veal. Flambé all the ingredients in the brandy. Stir in the white wine and simmer for 5 minutes. Stir in the cream and season according to taste. Serve immediately on a bed of rice or with tossed noodles.

Loin of Pork
with Apricot and Prunes

Serves eight

4½ lb (2 kg) loin of pork, boned and rolled
8 oz (225 g) dried apricots
8 oz (225 g) dried prunes
1 large onion, finely chopped
2 oz (50 g) butter
2 cups fine white breadcrumbs
2 oz (50 g) pistachio nuts
salt and pepper
ground cloves and nutmeg
2 cups orange juice
grated rind of 2 oranges
1 cup of port
cornflower in water

Set oven at 350°F (180°C, Gas 4). Unroll the pork and place on a large board. Prepare the stuffing. Chop the apricots and prunes and sauté with the onion and nuts in the butter. Season with salt and pepper, ground cloves and nutmeg. Remove from the heat and reserve 4 tablespoons of the mixture, stir the breadcrumbs into the remaining mixture, and moisten with a little orange juice. Spread the mixture onto the meat and roll up and secure with string.

Roast for 2 hours, basting frequently. After the first hour of cooking, pour the orange juice, zest and port over the pork with the reserved apricot mixture. Return to the oven. If the liquid reduces too much, add extra orange juice or stock. Remove the meat from the oven and carve. Thicken the sauce with the cornflower and pour over and around the meat.

Barbecued Spare Ribs in Ginger Sauce

Serves four

This is a very aromatic sauce and can be made well in advance and stored in a container in the fridge until needed. It could be used with chicken portions as well.

Approximately 2 lbs (900 g) spare ribs, depending on how meaty they
  are
1 cup tomato ketchup
1 teaspoon fresh grated ginger
2 tablespoons Worcestershire sauce
2 tablespoons lemon juice
1 teaspoon minced garlic
2 tablespoons clear honey
1 teaspoon grated coriander
salt and pepper

Set oven at 400°F (200°C, Gas 6). Marinate the ribs in the sauce made from all the above ingredients for as long as possible. Bake for 30 – 40 minutes, basting frequently.

Warm Fillet of Beef Salad

Choose your own quantities

fillet beef, sliced into julienne strips
butter for frying
emmental cheese, sliced into julienne strips
cleaned, young celery cut into similar lengths
halved walnuts
cooked beetroot, cut into julienne strips
young lettuce leaves
washed and trimmed watercress

Mustard Vinaigrette makes ¾ pint (450 ml)

4 teaspoons dijon mustard
salt and pepper
3 teaspoons sugar
mixed herbs
3½ tablespoons wine vinegar
½ pint (300 ml) olive oil
crushed garlic, if desired

Fill the salad bowl with the salad and watercress. Make the vinaigrette in a magimix or liquidiser by combining all the ingredients together and blending them until thick. Use what vinaigrette you need and keep the rest in the refrigerator for future use. Toss the vegetables, cheese and nuts in the vinaigrette and transfer to the salad bowl.

Fry the beef in the butter and then sprinkle the beef over the salad, toss and serve immediately.

Rosemary, New Potatoes and Roquefort Salad

Serves eight

This is delicious with cold meat, such as veal and lamb, and superb with grilled lamb chops or steak.

2 lb (900 g) scrubbed new potatoes
1 tablespoon Dijon mustard
salt and pepper
3 fl oz (90 ml) wine vinegar
1½ tablespoons fresh rosemary
9 fl oz (270 ml) olive oil
¼ lb (125 g) roquefort cheese, crumbled
1 sprig rosemary to garnish

Cook the new potatoes until tender and drain. Put the mustard, seasoning, rosemary, vinegar and oil in the liquidiser and blend until thick. Stir in the roquefort and pour all over the potatoes. Chill for several hours and garnish with the rosemary.

Tagliatelle Salad

Serves six

12 oz (350 g) fresh tagliatelle
1 full cup tunafish
mayonnaise to taste
garlic and chopped parsley
vinaigrette to taste
1 cup tinned white haricots beans, drained
fresh black pepper
½ pint (300 ml) whipped cream

Cook the tagliatelle and drain it. Mix in the other ingredients, sprinkle
with chopped parsley and serve very chilled.

Broad Bean, Mange-Tout and Bacon Salad

Serves 18 – 20 for a buffet. Divide the quantity by three to serve six

1½ lb (700 g) mange-touts
3 lb (1.4 kg) tender young broad beans
12 tomatoes, skinned, quartered and seeds removed
1½ lbs (700 g) back bacon, rinds removed
chopped parsley

Mustard vinaigrette recipe on page 100

Trim the mange-touts, blanch in salted boiling water for a few minutes, then blanch the broad beans for a few minutes. Drain and rinse them both in cold water. Cut the tomatoes in half again and mix all the vegetables in the vinaigrette.

Cook the bacon until crispy and cut into little pieces, toss the bacon with everything else, sprinkle with chopped parsley and serve.

Chestnut Purée

Serves eight

Purée vegetables have become very trendy now. So here are three
rather unusual ideas. Chestnut Purée is ideal for game recipes and
delicious with turkey at Christmas.

15½ oz (439 g) unsweetened Chestnut Purée
½ lb (225 g) potatoes, cooked and mashed
4 oz (125 g) butter, melted
¼ pint (150 ml) double cream
salt, pepper and grated nutmeg

Purée the chestnut with the potatoes and melted butter. Add the cream
and seasoning and remix the purée. Heat the mixture through and
serve.

Beetroot and Cumin Purée

Serves four

This purée is delicious with duck and provides a bright contrast of colour to roast pork or veal. You can easily make up your own purées, so
have fun – make three different purées and arrange them attractively
around the meat or game you are serving.

1 lb (450 g) cooked beetroot, peeled and finely sliced
1 onion, finely chopped
2 oz (50 g) butter
salt and pepper and ground cloves
cumin and crushed garlic to taste
¼ pint (150 ml) soured cream
2 glasses port

fresh mint to decorate

Cook the onion in the butter, cumin and garlic for 10 minutes until
transparent. Stir in the beetroot, port, salt, pepper and a little ground
cloves. Simmer for 5 minutes.

   Purée the mixture and reheat stirring in the sour cream and adjust
the seasoning. Serve in a dish decorated with fresh mint.

Potato, Leek and Garlic Purée

Serves six

This is delicious with casseroles or roast meats in winter. Alter the amount of garlic used to suit your own preference.

1 lb (450 g) leeks, cleaned and chopped
1 lb (450 g) potatoes, peeled and chopped
4 oz (125 g) butter
6 cloves crushed garlic
2 egg yolks
cream or milk
salt and pepper

Cook the potatoes and leeks in the butter with the garlic, until soft but not browned. Liquidize the mixture and season to taste. Beat the eggs in a little cream and beat into the mixture. Add more cream until you have the consistency you require.

Fried Potatoes with Rosemary

Serves four

These potatoes are delicious with any roast meat or sauté meat dishes.

1½ lbs (700 g) potatoes, halved and parboiled
3 tablespoons olive oil
1 oz (25 g) butter
2 cloves crushed garlic
2 sprigs rosemary
salt and pepper

Quarter the potato halves and sauté in frying pan with the garlic, oil, butter and rosemary until brown and crispy all over. Sprinkle with salt and pepper and serve with any lamb or veal dish.

New Potatoes in Orange Butter

Serves ten

These potatoes are delicious with hot salmon or trout for a summer dinner party.

2½ lbs (1200 g) new potoates
5 oz (150 g) butter
½ cup orange juice
grated rind of one orange
salt and pepper
fresh mint, to decorate

Cook the potatoes in boiling, salted water until tender and drain. Boil all the remaining ingredients together in a saucepan for 2 – 3 minutes and pour over the hot poatoes. Decorate with the mint.

Savoury Rice

Serves six

Use this recipe for any poultry, meat, vegetable or fish but use a suitable stock.

16 oz (453 g) patna or basmati rice
1½ pints (900 ml) hot fish stock (cubes are fine)
2 tablespoons olive oil
1 – 2 cloves crushed garlic
4 oz (125 g) chopped onion
2 oz (50 g) butter
salt and pepper

Set oven at 400°F (200°C, Gas 6). Wash the rice, changing the water 5 times and soak the rice for 20 minutes. Heat the oil and sauté the onion for 2 minutes. Add the garlic and rice and cook for 1 minute.

Pour the boiling stock over the rice and season with salt and pepper. Cover with a piece of buttered paper and a lid and cook in the oven for 20 minutes. Transfer the rice to a big dish and add knobs of butter with a fork. The rice can easily be reheated.

Baked Cucumber and Dill

Serves six

I always serve cucumber in this way with salmon or trout; it is excellent with veal too.

 2 cucumbers, peeled and cut into 2 inch (5 cm) sticks
 salt and black pepper
 white wine vinegar
 castor sugar
 fresh mint
 fresh or dried dill

Set oven at 325°F (160°C, Gas 3). Cover the cucumbers with salt and leave under a cloth for 20 minutes. Rinse the cucumber and pat dry with a clean cloth.

Arrange the cucumber in a large oven-proof dish and sprinkle with dill, pepper, vinegar and sugar. Cover with foil and bake for 30 minutes or until tender. Serve with sprigs of fresh mint.

Haricots Verts and Waterchestnuts

Serves four

You could cook these vegetables in a wok to accompany a Chinese meal, or you could steam the vegetables to accompany fish.

    8 oz (225 g) waterchestnuts, sliced
    8 oz (225 g) fresh or frozen haricots verts
    salt and pepper
    butter

Trim the fresh haricots verts. Cook the beans until just crunchy. Drain them and toss with the sliced chestnuts in butter and season to taste.

The Perfect Cheeseboard

All advice has been given by Paxton & Whitfield, cheesemongers since 1797.

Choosing a cheeseboard is expensive so have fun doing it! First decide on the theme of your cheeseboard; for example, either a board consisting of all types of cheeses, from the popular English to the uncommon French, or a selection that concentrates on only one or two varieties: for example all blue cheeses or all goat's milk cheeses.

Once this has been decided you have other options in front of you. A selection of cheeses from one country or perhaps one cheese from lots of countries. Then decide on colour and shape, hardness and softness. Also base your cheeses on a selection of old and new varieties, as some guests will certainly wish to see some well known names, but it is important to strike a happy medium. Be adventurous and insist that your guests do the same.

It is very important to buy the right quantity of cheese, as only a few cheeses keep well. Only get what you need for immediate consumption. Remember heavier cheeses will not be consumed in such quantities as the lighter varieties. As a general guide 2 oz (50 g) per person is about right.

The cheese should be in perfect condition when you buy it. Do not take the cheeses in and out of the fridge; this only does them harm. You can refrigerate a very smelly cheese, so as to stop it going off. Re-wrap cheeses to refrigerate.

Your cheeseboard should be based on your type of menu, smart or casual accordingly. If you have an rich dinner, have small light cheeses, if however you have a light menu, you have more scope to enjoy full flavoured cheeses.

For a small dinner party of eight, you should only need four cheeses, each one about ½ lb (225 g) in weight. Six cheeses should be enough for 10 – 12 people. I would choose a blue cheese, a British firm cheese, a goat cheese and a soft cheese like Brie or Camembert.

Bring the cheese out of the fridge to recover its room temperature at about the same time as you would bring out a red wine or port. Use a good selection of biscuits to accompany the cheese eg: plain biscuits for full flavoured cheese. Good quality fruit is essential with cheese.

Britain is probably best known for its hard cheeses but it has more recently produced a number of excellent soft cheeses. The hard cheeses vary so much in colour: the Windsor Red, for example, has delicate traces of elderberry wine while the traditional Sage Derby contains bright green sage leaves. Cheshire cheese is produced in red, white and blue; it could make an attractive cheeseboard on its own.

France on the other hand is better known for its soft cheeses. They are producing more than 1000 varieties at the moment. Some people find goat cheese too strong, but they do come in all sorts of fun shapes and colours and look good on a cheeseboard. Sheep's milk cheeses are now available in greater numbers; the best known is of course Roquefort. There are many blue cheeses on the market now from all over the world. Here is a rough guide to the six main categories.

1) *Unusual Blues:*

Roquefort is matured naturally in caves in the South of France. Its veins produce a lovely delicate flavour.

Mountain Gorgonzola, possibly the most famous of Italian cheeses, made in the Lombardy region. It is matured for about four months so that it becomes very rich.

2) *Goat's Milk Cheeses:*

These cheeses have gained popularity in the last few years. Most 'chevres' are made with unpasteurised milk. British cheeses are traditionally eaten young; they should be fresh and flaky in texture. Foreign ones become bitter as they age.

Bucheron is a general term for a long cylinder shaped cheese, usually sold by the pound. Made in France, it acquires a very goaty flavour. It has a closer texture than English cheese.

Lingot Ash is a brick shape cheese coated with edible ash. Some log or pyramid cheeses can be coated in fresh herbs or leaves. They weigh about 8 oz (225 g) each and are bought as whole cheeses.

Crottin is rather an unusual French Cheese, usually about 2½ oz (70 g). The French like to mature these cheeses to acquire a hard, blackened appearance, hence the name which literally translated means 'horse dung'! This is usually too strong for the English palate!

3) *Brie types of soft cheeses:*

Farmhouse Brie, also known as Brie de Meaux or Brie Fermier, is made with unpasteurised milk, which gives a stronger flavour than ordinary Brie. The rind gives a mottled brown colour to indicate its age.

Farmhouse Camembert is usually packed in more rustic boxes. The label should include the term 'lait cru' – raw milk. You can ripen a whole Camembert if you have plenty of time. Wedges of soft cheese do not ripen well.

St. Albray is more popular and easily recognised by its six sides and hole in the centre. It is mild, but tasty.

Neufchâtel is very similar to Brie and most often sold in a heart shape. it is also very mild.

4) *Triple Cream Cheeses:*

This term usually applies to cheese with 75% or more fat content. The following cheeses should be kept in a refrigerator.

Boursault is a small 5 oz (150 g) cheese, with a fresh, creamy flavour and texture; named after its inventor Monsieur Boursault.

5) *Specialist European Cheeses:*

Mature Gouda and Edam. Only the finest quality cheeses are selected for the lengthy maturing process, which may be up to one year. The rind of both should be yellow wax.

Gaperon is a dome-shaped cheese from the Auvergne region of France and has been made for centuries; based on an excess of milk and garlic in the area. The cheese is tied with raffia which adds to its appeal.

Mature Cheddar. A good farmhouse cheddar should be matured for at least 18 months to acquire its strong flavour. Wrap it in foil and keep cool to prevent the cheese from sweating.

6) *Washed Rind Cheese:*

This term applies to cheeses that have been washed in a liquid such as wine, which makes the rind very aromatic.

Chocolate and Blackcherry Trifle

Serves eight

This pudding is ideal for family Sunday lunch. If there are young children, I tend to cut down on the Kirsch, but it's just as delicious.

1 × 2 egg chocolate sponge, or a bought sponge
12 oz (340 g) black cherry jam
kirsch
½ pint (300 ml) whipped cream
15 oz (425 g) tinned black cherries
1 pint very thick custard, flavoured with vanilla
3.5 oz (100 g) dark chocolate

To make chocolate caraque: gently melt the chocolate in a bowl over hot water and then spread over a marble slab. When it has cooled, scrape the chocolate off the slab with a palette knife into thick curls.

Line a glass bowl with most of the sponge and sprinkle with kirsch. Melt the jam with some kirsch and spread over the sponge, reserving enough for the remaining sponge. Mix the custard with half the cream and pour over the sponge. Remove the stones from the cherries, cut them in half and spoon them over the custard. Cover with the remaining sponge and cream and decorate with the chocolate caraque.

Stuffed Pears in Chocolate Tulips

Serves six

Everything except the chocolate tulips may be made a day in advance.

6 small pears
1 pint (600 ml) water
½ lb (225 g) castor sugar
1 slice lemon peel

Chocolate Filling

2 oz (50 g) dark chocolate, softened
2 oz (50 g) ground almonds
1 teaspoon rum or brandy
½ oz (12 g) butter, softened
1 teaspoon double cream

Sabayon Sauce

2 egg yolks
2 oz (50 g) castor sugar
vanilla essence
2 oz (50 g) melted chocolate
10 fl oz (300 ml) double cream

Chocolate Tulips

2 oz (50 g) butter
2 oz (50 g) icing sugar
1 egg white, stiffly beaten
2 oz (50 g) flour
vanilla essence
3.5 oz (100 g) melted dark chocolate

Set oven at 400°F (200°C, Gas 6). Peel the pears but leave the stalks intact. Poach pears in a syrup, made from water, sugar and lemon peel, until tender but firm. Drain and chill. Make the sauce by mixing the egg yolks and sugar together in a magimix. Bring the cream to the boil. Pour the hot cream into the eggs and sugar and mix thoroughly. Transfer the custard to a saucepan and stir over low heat until it coats the back of the spoon. Add the vanilla and chocolate and chill. Keep covered under greaseproof paper.

Make the tulips next: beat the butter and icing sugar together in a bowl over hot water. When it is thick and creamy beat the flour into the mixture, incorporate the vanilla and egg white. Chill for 2 hours. Grease a baking tray or use a non-stick one.

Make the biscuits paper thin or it will be difficult to mould them into shape. Pipe or spread the mixture on to the tray in flower shapes about 3 inches (7.6 cm) wide. Make only a few at a time because they will spread. Cook for 5 minutes or less, just allowing them to brown around the edges; immediately mould the flowers into a tulip shape so that they can hold a pear. I usually use a large ramekin. When they are cool, paint them on the outside with melted chocolate, this helps to keep them crisp. Remove the cores from the pears and pat dry with a clean cloth. Stuff the pears with the filling. Mix the chocolate, almonds, rum, butter and cream and beat them together until smooth. Flatten the bottoms of the pears if necessary, so that they can stand upright in the tulips. Pour a little sauce into the centre of each plate. Put each pear into a tulip and place on the plates, pour over the remaining sauce and serve immediately.

Caramel and Pear Terrine

Serves ten

This is an exceptional pudding – the pear mousse is a very subtle contrast to the caramel mousse. The sauce compliments the flavour of both.

Caramel Mousse

1 × 14.1 oz (400 g) tin condensed milk, boiled for 3½ hours, unopened, in a saucepan, keep topping the pan up with boiling water.
½ pint (300 ml) double cream whipped
½ oz (11 g) gelatine dissolved in hot water
2 egg whites, stiffly beaten
vanilla essence

Pear Mousse

6 pears, peeled and chopped
10 fl oz (300 ml) sweet white wine
very good Cognac for flavour
2 oz (50 g) sugar
lemon juice to prevent colouring
½ oz (11 g) gelatine dissolved in hot water
½ pint (300 ml) double cream, whipped
2 egg whites, stiffly beaten

Caramel Decoration

4 oz (125 g) castor sugar
3 tablespoons water

extra white wine and lemon juice for the sauce

Butter a 9 inch (23 cm) loaf tin and line with grease-proof paper. Poach the pears in the wine and sugar and lemon juice until soft. Cool and liquidise. Add Cognac to taste. Keep ⅓ of the purée to one side for the sauce. Stir the gelatine into the ⅔ quantity of purée. As the mixture starts to set, fold in the cream and finally the egg whites. Leave in a cool place while you make the caramel mousse.

Scrape out the caramel from the cold tin and mix with the vanilla essence and stir in the gelatine. Fold in the cream and egg whites. Carefully spread half the mixture over the base of the tin – freeze for 5 minutes. Carefully spoon the pear mousse over the caramel layer and freeze for 10 minutes. Cover the mousses with the remaining caramel. Smooth over and chill until firmly set. Alternatively divide into two layers only.

Make the sauce by stiring more wine and lemon juice into the purée according to taste. You only need one spoonful per person.

Dip the loaf tin in hot water and turn onto a serving plate. Peel off the paper and decorate with chopped caramel. For an extra smart dinner party you can pipe rosettes of cream along the terrine. Alternatively, for a touch of nouvelle cuisine, slice the terrine onto each plate and surround with sauce, and decorate with caramel.

Mango and Kiwi Tartlets

Serves six

Mango skins maybe green or red depending on the variety. They should be tender to touch, keep in a warm place until needed. Use tinned mangoes in preference to unripe fruit

1 large frozen shortcrust pastry
or 14 oz (375 g) homemade
pastry

Orange Cream

¼ pint (150 ml) double cream,
 whipped
finely grated zest of one orange
juice of ¼ orange, strained
1 dessertspoon sifted icing sugar

Fruit Filling

1 large ripe mango
3 ripe kiwi fruit

Glaze

3 tablespoons apricot or guava
 jam
2 tablespoons kirsch

Roll out the pastry and line 12 tartlet tins. Bake the pastry blind, until crisp and golden. Cool on a wire rack.

Cut the mango flesh into neat little slices and peel and slice the kiwi fruit. Make the orange cream by mixing all the ingredients together and fill each tartlet with the cream. Arrange the fruit over the cream. Warm the jam and the kirsch together in a small saucepan, cool slightly, and glaze each tartlet. Chill before serving.

Langue de Chat aux Fraises

Serves six

The presentation of this mouth-watering pudding is very definitely influenced by nouvelle cuisine, with its small, neat appearance and the classic arrangement of sauce.

4 oz (125 g) icing sugar, sifted
4 oz (125 g) butter
2 egg whites
4 oz (125 g) flour
vanilla essence
½ pint (300 ml) cream, whipped
2 punnets of strawberries

Strawberry Coulis

12 oz (35 g) strawberries
icing sugar to taste

Set oven at 400°F (200°C, Gas 6). Cream the sugar and butter until white and creamy. Beat in vanilla and stir in the egg whites. Very carefully fold in the flour. Spread the mixture over a non-stick baking sheet. Bake for 5 minutes. Cut biscuit whilst warm into 2 × 3 inch (5 × 7.5 cm) rectangles. Whip the cream.

Make the strawberry coulis: purée the strawberries with the icing sugar. Reserve 6 strawberries. Sandwich the rectangles with the remaining strawberries, halved, and the whipped cream.

Sprinkle icing sugar over the top of each biscuit. Set on plates with the strawberry coulis spooned all around them. Use whole strawberries to decorate. If you are feeling very adventurous you can pour a tiny trickle of double cream all around the edge of the coulis and very carefully with a teaspoon make tiny feather patterns or swirls in the cream.

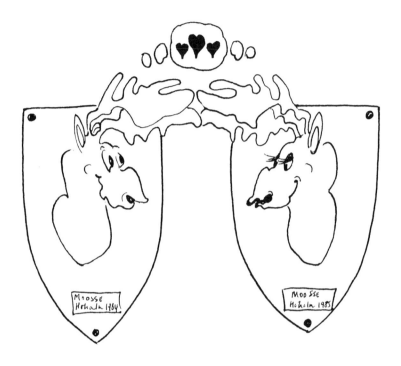

'Passion Moose!'

Passion Fruit Mousse

Serves six

This sounds very exotic, but it is very easy to make, and it is rather fun
to use an unusual tropical fruit for a change.

6 large passion fruit
6 egg yolks
6 egg whites, stiffly beaten
juice of one lemon
grated rind of half an orange
2 tablespoons cold water
1 tablespoon gelatine
2 tablespoons Orange Curaçao
4 oz (125 g) castor sugar
10 fl oz (300 ml) double cream, whipped
extra whipped cream and some roasted mixed nuts to decorate

Cut the passion fruit in half, scoop the pips out and push them through a
sieve and discard the seeds. Separate the eggs and carefully cook the
egg yolks with the passion fruit and lemon juice, Curaçao and sugar
over hot water until it coats the back of the spoon. Add the gelatine
dissolved in the water. Transfer the mixture to a china bowl and chill in
the refrigerator.

In another bowl, add the orange rind to the cream and fold into the
cooled custard. Fold in the egg whites, carefully pour the mousse into a
soufflé dish and chill for 6 hours. Decorate with rosettes of cream and
the nuts.

The passion fruit sauce on page 131 is a colourful compliment to the
mousse. Serve it separately in a sauceboat.

Sharon Fruit Timbale in Two Fruit Sauce

Serves six

This extraordinary fruit from Brazil has a very unusual and smooth taste. Keep the fruit in a warm place to ripen for 2 – 4 days before use, as they seldom seem ripe enough in the shops.

4 Sharon fruit, very ripe
3 dessertspoons frozen concentrated orange juice
A little Orange Curaçao
½ oz (11 g) gelatine dissolved in hot water
7 fl oz (200 ml) double cream, whipped

Sauces

14 oz (375 g) tin strawberries in syrup
15 oz (400 g) tin apricots in syrup
18 fresh mint leaves

Peel the Sharon fruit and slice the fruit into a magimix. Purée the fruit, stir in the orange juice, Orange Curaçao and gelatine. Fold in the double cream and divide the mixture into 6 ramekins. Chill for 3 hours.

Now prepare the sauces. Purée the strawberries in their syrup and chill. Purée the apricots in their syrup and chill.

To assemble: first spoon the apricot purée over half the plate, then spoon the strawberry purée over the other half so that they meet in the centre of the plate. Dip the ramekins in boiling hot water for a few seconds, and turn out on to the centre of the plate. Lay a mint leaf across the mousse and arrange the leaves at the top of the plate where the sauces join.

Mango Ice Cream

Serves eight

If you use fresh mangoes, they must be ripe; otherwise use tinned mangoes.

    4 egg yolks
    9 fl oz (250 ml) single cream
    ½ teaspoon vanilla essence
    ½ pint (300 ml) double cream, whipped
    4 fresh mangoes
    juice of half a lemon
    ⅔ cup of sugar
    kiwi fruit, strawberries, mango and fresh mint to decorate

Beat the egg yolks and sugar until frothy. Heat the single cream and combine with the egg mixture. Pour into a saucepan and cook gently, stirring constantly until the custard is thick. Add the vanilla and cool thoroughly.

Purée the mangoes with the lemon juice and stir into the custard. Freeze until very cold, then fold in the whipped cream. Beat occasionally during freezing time.

To present a masterpiece! Peel and slice the mangoes and kiwi fruit and halve the strawberries. Arrange the mint and all the fruit around the plates with small oval scoops of ice cream, surrounded by the sauce.

Mango and Passion Fruit Sauce

    425 g tin mangoes in syrup
    4 ripe passion fruit
    Orange Curaçao, to taste

Purée the mangoes in a magimix and scrape the pips from the passion fruit into the purée. Flavour with the Orange Curaçao and chill. Pour the sauce around the ice cream.

Triple Sorbet Paradise

Serves eight

This a delightful picture of colours which contrast brilliantly with the bright red sauce. This is easy and can be frozen weeks in advance.

Guava Sorbet

285 g tin guava halves in syrup
a little lemon juice
4 tablespoons water
3 tablespoons castor sugar
orange blossom water

Lychee Sorbet

425 g tin lychees in syrup
a little lemon juice
4 tablespoons water
3 tablespoons castor sugar

Melon Sorbet

1 ripe, medium sized melon
7 tablespoons water
5 tablespoons castor sugar
1 tablespoon lemon juice

Strawberry sauce

425 g tin strawberries in syrup
fresh mint to decorate

Make the melon sorbet first: dissolve the sugar in the water and boil until it becomes syrupy. Cool in the saucepan. Remove the seeds from the melon and scrape out the flesh. Blend the melon and syrup with the lemon juice in the liquidiser until smooth. Freeze until mushy. Blend the sorbet in the liquidiser again so that it is smooth and return to the freezer.

Now blend the guava halves in their syrup with the lemon juice and orange blossom water until smooth. Sieve the purée and remove the pips. Make a syrup with the water and sugar and stir it into the guava pulp. Freeze until mushy, beat with a fork for a few minutes so that the sorbet is smooth and return it to the freezer.

Liquidise the lychees in their syrup with the lemon juice. Make a syrup as above with the sugar and water and stir it into the lychee purée. Freeze until mushy. Blend in a food processor until very soft and smooth and return to the freezer. Liquidise the strawberries with their syrup and keep chilled.

To assemble the sorbets: spoon the sauce over the centre of each plate. Arrange a few leaves of fresh mint with any other fruit available. Carefully shape 1 spoonful of each sorbet onto the sauce and serve.

Marron Iced Meringues in Raspberry Coulis

Serves eight

These delicious ice cream meringues can be made well in advance and kept until needed. The sauce can be frozen in a separate container.

4 egg whites, stiffly beaten to form soft peaks
8 oz (225 g) vanilla sugar, sieved
Bakewell paper

Marron Ice Cream

5 egg yolks
4 oz (125 g) sugar
½ pint (300 ml) scalded milk
½ pint (300 ml) double cream, whipped
8 oz (225 g) unsweetened chestnut purée
chopped marron glacé, if available
vanilla pod or essence
1 tablespoon Cognac if desired

Raspberry Coulis

16 oz (450 g) ripe raspberries or 2 × 385 g tins raspberries in syrup
3 oz (75 g) castor sugar
juice of 1 lemon
raspberry liqueur

Decoration

¾ pint (350 ml) whipped cream, very cold
8 caramalised chestnuts or marrons glacés

Make the meringues and spoon 8 × 2 inches (5 cm) circles on Bakewell paper and then another 8 × 1½ inches (3.8 cm) circles beside them. Flatten the tops and bake in a very low heat, about 250°F (130°C, Gas ½), until crisp but not coloured. Keep the meringues in an air tight container until needed.

Make the ice cream: beat the egg yolks and sugar together in a magimix, pour in the hot milk with the motor running and transfer the custard into a saucepan. Cook the custard over low heat until thick, but do not boil. A split vanilla pod can be used during cooking or vanilla essence but don't forget to remove the pod afterwards!

Return the custard to the magimix and blend in the chestnut purée and cognac. Chill the custard and fold in the whipped cream, freeze for a few hours before folding in the chopped marron.

Make the raspberry coulis: purée the raspberries with the liqueur, lemon and sugar. Sieve to remove the pips and chill.

To assemble: spoon some chestnut ice cream onto the larger meringue and cover with the smaller meringue, and smooth into a mountain shape. Cover with whipped cream and smooth with a palette knife. Decorate with marron. Keep frozen until about 20 minutes before needed.

To serve: set each meringue in the centre of each plate and surround each one with the raspberry coulis. Decorate with a few extra raspberries if you have some.

Baileys Ice Cream

Serves sixteen

This recipe is delightfully alcoholic and the sauce is even more so! If you do not have time to make the sauce just serve the ice cream with lots of grated chocolate.

6 egg yolks
6 egg whites
6 oz (175 g) castor sugar
1 teaspoon vanilla essence
1 pint (600 ml) milk

1 pint (600 ml) double cream,
  whipped
10 tablespoons Baileys Irish
  Cream
3.5 oz (100 g) dark chocolate,
  melted and kept warm

Bring the milk to the boil. Beat the egg yolks with the sugar until light and fluffy. Stir in the hot milk and cook gently until the custard coats the back of the spoon, add the vanilla essence and leave to cool.

Stir in the Baileys and freeze for an hour or so, beating occasionally to keep the ice cream smooth. Fold in the whipped cream and return to the freezer until nearly frozen but still manageable.

Then dribble the melted chocolate into the ice cream and fold in the whipped egg whites. Keep frozen until needed. Serve decorated with grated chocolate and accompany with the following sauce.

Hazelnut Crème Anglaise

4 egg yolks
⅔ cup of sugar
2 cups double cream

½ cup roasted hazelnuts,
  finely chopped
Cognac to taste
lots of Baileys Irish Cream

Beat the eggs and sugar together. Heat the cream and gradually whisk in to the eggs. Cook the custard until thick but do not boil. Stir in the hazelnuts and chill. Pour in the Irish cream and Cognac, a little at a time until the sauce is very boozy and delicious!

Pears in Raspberry Sauce

Serves six

This can be made the day before needed; keep spooning the sauce over the pears, this will give them a pretty pink tinge.

6 large ripe pears
½ pint (300 ml) medium dry white wine
1 strip lemon peel
4 oz (125 g) castor sugar
¼ pint (150 ml) water

Raspberry Sauce

8 oz (225 g) ripe raspberries, hulled
4 oz (125 g) castor sugar

Dissolve the sugar with the water, wine and lemon peel and make a syrup. Peel the pears and poach them upright in the syrup until soft but firm.

Make the raspberry sauce by blending the raspberries in the liquidizer with the sugar and a little of the syrup, sieve and chill. Remove the pears from the remaining syrup and chill. Pour the sauce over the pears and keep chilled until ready to serve.

Fresh Fig Tart

Serves four

Buy a ready made sweet pastry case, now available in most super-markets or make one: The recipe is as follows.

Paté Sucrée

4 oz (125 g) plain flour
2 oz (50 g) caster sugar
2 oz (50 g) butter
2 egg yolks
pinch of salt

Work all the ingredients together on a cool, floured surface, knead until firm and chill for 1 hour. Line a 6 inch (15 cm) flan ring.
　　Bake the pastry blind until crisp and golden. Cool on a wire rack.

Filling

6 large, fresh, ripe figs, peeled and halved
2 oz (50 g) cream cheese
1 dessertspoon icing sugar, sifted
vanilla essence
5 fl oz (150 ml) whipped cream
4 oz (125 g) redcurrant jelly, or any other fruit jelly
1 dessertspoon hot water

Melt the redcurrant jelly with the water and leave to cool. Mix the icing sugar with the cream cheese and fold in the whipped cream. Flavour with vanilla essence and spoon in the pastry case. Completely cover with fresh figs and glaze with the cool redcurrant jelly. Keep chilled until ready to serve.

Ginger and Treacle Tart

Serves six

This is a sturdy winter pudding, ideal for shooting parties as it can be frozen and re-heated.

Buy a ready made shortcrust pastry case or make it yourself.

Shortcrust Pastry:

8 oz (225 g) plain flour
½ level teaspoon salt
2 oz (50 g) lard
2 oz (50 g) butter
a little cold water

Filling:

Juice of half a lemon

6 rounded tablespoons golden syrup
3 tablespoons fresh white breadcrumbs
2 level tablespoons stem ginger syrup
2 heaped tablespoons chopped stem ginger

Whipped cream to serve

Set oven at 400°F (200°C, Gas 6). Make the pastry and chill for half an hour. Roll the pastry out and line a greased 9 inch (23 cm) flan dish. Make the filling by mixing all the ingredients together and spoon into the pastry case.
    Bake for 30 – 35 minutes, serve warm or cold.

Crêpes aux Amandes

Serves four-six

These are very easy and alcoholic crêpes. You can make the mixture in a magimix in no time at all. They freeze very well and can be heated up dotted with butter in the oven or tossed in butter in a frying pan.

½ Pint (300 ml) Crêpe Mixture:

4 oz (125 g) plain flour
½ pint (300 ml) milk
1 egg yolk
1 whole egg
2 tablespoons melted butter
pinch of salt

brandy, to flame crêpes

Filling:

3.5 oz (100 g) ground almonds
4 oz (125 g) unsalted butter
almond essence
Grand Marnier
11 oz (300 g) icing sugar – sifted

Make the pancakes in a magimix and leave the mixture to stand for 30 minutes. Meanwhile make the filling: mix all the ingredients together, adding the essence and liqueur to your individual taste. The mixture should be very smooth and creamy.

Make the crêpes and fill each one with the mixture. Fold them into triangles and reheat. Flame in brandy in front of your guests.

Hot Ginger Soufflé

Serves eight

I was always very nervous of making sweet soufflés, but I often do them now because they can be prepared in advance and I just whisk up the egg whites as the main course is being served.

    2 × 1 pint (600 ml) soufflé dishes
    2 – 3 tablespoons castor sugar for dusting the dish
    butter for greasing the dishes
    2 oz (50 g) butter
    2 tablespoons flour
    2 tablespoons cornflour
    ¾ pint (450 ml) warm milk
    2 tablespoons sugar
    3 tablespoons stem ginger syrup
    3 tablespoons chopped stem ginger
    4 egg yolks
    6 egg whites
    tiny pinch salt

Set oven at 400°F (200°C, Gas 6). Grease the soufflé dishes with butter and dust with sugar. Melt the butter in a saucepan over low heat, add the flours and stir for one minute. Remove from heat and cool a little. Add warm milk and stir until smooth. Return to heat and bring to boil, for thirty seconds, remove from heat and stir in the sugar, ginger and syrup. Beat in the egg yolks one by one, stir in the salt.

Transfer the mixture into a large bowl. Whisk the egg whites stiffly, fold 1 large spoonful into the mixture and then fold in the rest with a cutting motion.

Turn the mixture into the soufflé dishes. Wrap a thick band of greaseproof paper around each dish and secure with string.

Turn the oven down to 375°F (190°C, Gas 5). Bake the soufflés for 30 minutes. Remove the collars of paper and serve immediately.

Advice on Choosing Port

Vintage Port is in a world of its own. The 'must'—fermenting grape juice—is added to a brandy base, which has a high enough alcohol content to kill the yeast. Hence the natural sugar in the must is not fermented dry, but remains to give port its unique flavour.

The great names—Taylor, Warre, Graham, to name only my favourites—produce fine wines every time they declare a Vintage. In some cases it can be nine years between declaring a new vintage worthy of bearing a producer's name. Drinking now, and for some time to come, are the 55's, 60's, 63's and 66's. Lay down 77's if you can find them. 1975 is also useful as a youngish vintage drinking well now.

Late bottled Vintage port is a good buy – after four years in cask it matures more quickly than Vintage port, and has 'thrown' most of its sediment before bottling.

Crusted port is a lesser wine – being a blend of various wines, but can age in the bottle quickly, so a good drink does no have to sit in the bottle for 10 – 15 years before drinking.

Look out for old tawny port as well – this will have some very old wines in the blend – now one can see various producers aging them from between 5 – 40 years in cask.

The Coffee Pot

The green coffee beans arrive in huge 60 kilo jute or sisal sacks from all over the world. All the beans are treated in different ways, some are washed and some are left in their parchment for roasting. The beans are roasted very quickly according to how dark they are required, but usually for 10 – 12 minutes in a sealed drum heated from the outside.

It takes about 3 months for the coffee beans to get to the customer, by the time the coffee has been processed, exported and stored in warehouses; so here is some advice on storing your coffee.

Storing Coffee

Keep the coffee beans in the smallest darkest jar you have, thus allowing as little air as possible into the jar. This should keep up to a month before losing its flavour. Ground coffee only lasts up to 3 – 4 days, but actually starts to deteriorate as soon as oxygen reaches it during the grinding process. Do not freeze coffee beans as they merely become damp.

Grinding Coffee Beans

For a Percolator	Grind Coarsely
For a Cafetier	Grind a little less coarsely
For a Jug and Strainer...........	about the same
For a Filter	Grind finely
For an Expresso....................	Grind very finely
For a Turkish Coffee	Grind as fine as flour

Choosing Coffee Beans

In this country we tend to start the day off with milder blends of coffee and we gradually progress to the darker, stronger roasts after dinner.

FOR EXAMPLE: After lunch use something not too thick, like a Guatamalan or Colombian bean or stick to your normal breakfast blends.

After dinner blends usually need something to cut through the taste of all the food. So use a blend of Kenya which is very strong with Brazilian or something similar.

The 'Continental' Roast which has a very bitter/sweet taste is used for expresso coffee. It is very black and glossy because of the very high degree of roast which coats the beans in their own cafol oil.

The 'Java Old Government' bean has a lovely musty flavour as it will have been kept for 5 years in Indonesia before being exported here, it makes a delicious cup of coffee.

Experimenting with Coffee

The most important thing to remember about coffee is that it totally depends on the type of water in your area.

FOR SOFT WATER USE: Hard, sharp, acidic Kenyan beans
FOR HARD WATER USE: Soft Central American beans

I would like to thank 'AROMA' coffee shop, St Mary's Place, Shrewsbury, for all their help.

The Anchovy Twist

Anchovy Twists

Serves six

These are an ideal savoury to accompany the port, and they can be stored in an air-tight container and reheated.

1.75 oz (50 g) anchovy fillets
4 oz (125 g) plain flour
salt and cayenne pepper
2 oz (50 g) butter
2 oz (50 g) Cheddar cheese, grated
1 egg yolk beaten with
2 – 3 teaspoons cold water
1 beaten egg for glazing

Set oven at 350°F (180°C, Gas 4). Sift the flour, a pinch of salt and cayenne pepper into a wide bowl. Cut up the butter and rub into the flour with finger tips until the mixture resembles breadcrumbs. Mix in the grated cheese and beaten egg yolk. Knead the dough lightly on a floured surface and chill.

Roll the pastry out to ¼ inch (6 mm) thick and cut into strips. Take each anchovy fillet and cut in half, lengthwise, and wrap around each strip of pastry, twisting it so the anchovy is held firmly in place. Brush lightly with beaten egg to glaze.

Cook in oven until golden brown and crisp, about 15 – 20 minutes.

Hot Pâté and Mushroom Toasts

Serves six

This is very quick and easy so that you can nip into the kitchen after the main course and put it all together.

> 6 slices bread, crusts removed
> butter and fresh thyme
> 2 × 2.2 oz (62 g) tins le Parfait Pâté
> 4 tablespoons sherry
> 2 tablespoons double cream
> 12 oz (350 g) mushrooms, peeled
> nutmeg, salt and pepper
> parsley to decorate

To save time, prepare the pâté and cook the mushrooms in advance. Reheat the mushrooms as you make the toast.

Mash the pâté with the cream and sherry, season if necessary. Finely slice the mushrooms and sauté for a few minutes in butter and thyme and sprinkle with the sherry. Toast the bread and cut into equal sized fingers. Spread the pâté over each finger of toast and cover with plenty of mushrooms.

Decorate with a little bit of parsley and serve immediately.

Asparagus and Scrambled Egg Tartlets

Serves six

1 large frozen shortcrust pastry or 14 oz (375 g) homemade pastry
6 eggs
4 oz (125 g) Petit Suisse or Jockey cream cheese
salt and pepper
12 asparagus tips
2 oz (50 g) butter

Set oven at 400°F (200°C, Gas 6). To make things easier for yourself, bake blind 12 small pastry cases in a greased tartlet tin. Store in a sealed container in a cool place.

Heat the pastry cases through during dinner and leave the egg mixture ready to use.

Mix the eggs, cream cheese and seasoning together in a bowl. Poach the asparagus in boiling salted water. Drain and keep the asparagus warm wrapped in foil.

At the last minute melt the butter in a saucepan and make the scrambled egg with the egg mixture. Divide it between the 12 pastry cases. Top with a piece of asparagus and serve immediately.

Roquefort Mille-Feuilles

Serves six

13.5 oz (375 g) frozen puff pastry
8 oz (225 g) Roquefort cheese
3.5 oz (100 g) butter, softened
2 tablespoons, freshly chopped parsley
2 egg yolks
4 tablespoons double cream
salt and pepper
1 beaten egg
grated parmesan and cayenne pepper
watercress to decorate

Set oven at 400°F (200°C, Gas 6). Divide the pastry into three, roll it into rectangles. Prick two of the rectangles with a fork and chill all three for 30 minutes.

Make the filling: in a magimix beat the cheese, butter, seasoning, parsley, egg yolks and cream. Glaze the unpricked rectangle of pastry with the beaten egg and sprinkle with the grated parmesan and cayenne. Bake for 12 minutes and cool on a wire rack. Bake the other two unglazed rectangles and cool.

Turn the oven down to 375°F (190°C, Gas 5). Spread the cheese mixture over the two unglazed rectangles of pastry and top with the glazed one. Trim edges and sides and bake the mille-feuille for 10 minutes or until heated through. Decorate with watercress and serve immediately.

Stuffed Baked Mushrooms

Serves eight

These are very easy and can be made hours in advance and kept under clingfilm in a cool place until needed.

2 medium sized mushrooms per person, approx. 3 in (7.6 cm) wide
2 oz (50 g) butter, finely diced
8 oz (225 g) ricotta cheese
8 oz (225 g) minced or finely chopped ham
fresh thyme
salt and pepper
2½ oz (60 g) breadcrumbs
2 oz (50 g) grated parmesan

Set oven at 400°F (200°C, Gas 6). Wash and trim the mushrooms and pat dry with a clean cloth. Fill them with a mixture of the ricotta, ham, thyme, salt and pepper, breadcrumbs, parmesan and butter and bake in a buttered oven-proof dish for 15 minutes or until the breadcrumbs are golden brown and the mushrooms are soft.

'Tempting Truffles!'

Coffee and Almond Truffles

For approximately 30 truffles

If you are a dedicated chocolate lover, here are 3 recipes for you to try!
Everyone is always impressed by hand-made chocolates, so it is well
worth the effort.

>   11 oz (300 g) dark chocolate
>   9 oz (250 g) icing sugar, sifted
>   2 teaspoons powdered instant coffee
>   3.5 oz (100 g) ground almonds
>   2 tablespoons cream
>   Cocoa powder for rolling the truffles
>   3 tablespoons rum

Melt chocolate in a bowl over hot water. Stir in icing sugar, coffee,
almonds, cream and rum. Cool and roll into little balls in the palm of
your hand and coat with cocoa.

Keep refrigerated until needed.

Orange Liqueur Truffles

For approximately 28 truffles

8 oz (225 g) icing sugar, sifted
8 oz (225 g) orange flavoured chocolate
1 egg yolk
1 oz (25 g) butter
2 tablespoons Amaretto or Grand Marnier
1 tablespoon double cream
3 oz (75 g) chocolate vermicelli or cocoa

Melt the chocolate in a small bowl over a saucepan of hot water. Remove from the heat and stir in the egg, butter, liqueur and cream. Beat the icing sugar into the mixture until firm enough to handle. Chill if necessary.

Shape into balls and coat with cocoa. Keep chilled for storage.

Chocolate Coated Almonds

Suitable for a large dinner party

3.5 oz (100 g) packet blanched almonds
7 oz (200 g) plain chocolate or milk chocolate

Melt the chocolate in a double saucepan, or in a bowl over hot water.
Dip the almonds in the chocolate one by one, and lay them on waxed
paper while the chocolate sets.

Alternatively used roasted, skinned hazelnuts or a mixture of both.

'The Hectic Hostess!'

Three Hectic Hostess Menus

Here are 3 menus for frantic ladies rushing back from work to give a dinner party! All the ingredients can be bought the day before.

The Passion Fruit Mousse should be made the day before; the Petits Fours are available from most shops and bakers.

Menu 1

Sara's Tuna Fish Soup
Sauté Chicken and Courgettes
New Potatoes and Mint
Stuffed Baked Mushrooms

Menu 2

Avocado in Redcurrant Vinaigrette
Fillet steak with Hazelnut Hollandaise Sauce
Fried Potatoes in Rosemary
Passion Fruit Mousse and Petits Fours

Menu 3

Proscuitto and Cheese Rolls with Brown Bread and Butter
Chicken in Garlic Crisps
A Green Salad
Pears in Raspberry Sauce

A Summer Hamper

This is the perfect picnic for a party at Glynebourne or an evening racing at Windsor. Everything can be prepared the day before.

Seafood Terrine and French Bread
Cold Veal and Ham Paupiettes
Broad Bean, Mange-Tout and Bacon Salad
Rosemary, New Potato and Roquefort Salad
Mango and Kiwi Tartlets